Granville Barker's
Prefaces to Shakespeare

A MIDSUMMER NIGHT'S DREAM
THE WINTER'S TALE
TWELFTH NIGHT

Foreword by
Richard Eyre

NICK HERN BOOKS

First published in this collected paperback edition in 1993 jointly by
Nick Hern Books Limited, 14 Larden Road, London W3 7ST
and the Royal National Theatre, London,
by arrangement with Batsford.

Preface to A Midsummer Night's Dream. Originally published in 1914,
second version 1924
Preface to The Winter's Tale originally published in 1912
Preface to Twelfth Night originally published in 1912

Set in 10/11 Baskerville by Pure Tech Corporation, Pondicherry
(India)
Printed in Australia by
Australian Print Group

A CIP catalogue record for this book is available from the British
Library

ISBN 1 85459 177 0

Shakespeare Alive!

The history of the theatre in England in this century can be told largely through the lives and work of two men: George Bernard Shaw and Harley Granville Barker, a triple-barrelled cadence of names that resonates like the ruffling of the pages of a large book in a silent public library. One was a brilliant polemicist who dealt with certainties and assertions and sometimes, but not often enough, breathed life into his sermons; the other a committed sceptic who started from the premise that the only thing certain about human behaviour was that nothing was certain. Both, however, possessed a passionate certainty about the importance of the theatre and the need to revise its form, its content, and the way that it was managed. Shaw was a playwright, critic and pamphleteer, Barker a playwright, director and actor.

The Voysey Inheritance is, at least in my opinion, Granville Barker's best play: a complex web of family relationships, a fervent but never unambiguous indictment of a world dominated by the mutually dependent obsessions of greed, class, and self-deception. It's also a virtuoso display of stagecraft: the writer showing that as director he can handle twelve speaking characters on stage at one time, and that as actor he can deal with the most ambitious and unexpected modulations of thought and feeling. The 'inheritance' of the Voyseys is a legacy of debt, bad faith, and bitter family dissension. Edward's father has, shortly before his death, revealed that he has been cheating the family firm of solicitors for many years, as his father had for many years before that. Towards the end of the play Edward Voysey, the youngest son, confronts the woman he loves:

> EDWARD.   Why wouldn't he own the truth to me about himself?
>
> BEATRICE.   Perhaps he took care not to know it. Would you have understood?
>
> EDWARD.   Perhaps not. But I loved him.
>
> BEATRICE.   That would silence a bench of judges.

Shaw would have used the story to moralise and polemicise. He might have had the son hate the father; he might have had him forgive him; he might have had him indict him as a paradigm of capitalism; he would never have said he loved him.

Everybody needs a father, or, failing that, a father-figure. He may be a teacher, a prophet, a boss, a priest perhaps, a political leader, a friend, or, sometimes, if you are very lucky, the real one. If you can't find a father you must invent him. In some ways, not altogether trivial, Granville Barker is something of a father-figure for me. He's a writer whom I admire more than any twentieth-century English writer before the sixties – Chekhov with an English accent; he's the first modern British director; he's the real founder of the National Theatre and, in his *Prefaces*, he's a man who, alone amongst Shakespearean commentators before Jan Kott, believed in the power of Shakespeare on stage.

There was a myth that Granville Barker was the natural son of Shaw. He was certainly someone whom Shaw could, in his awkward way, cherish and admire, educate and castigate. When Barker fell wildly in love ('in the Italian manner' as Shaw said) with Helen Huntington, an American millionairess, he married her, acquired a hyphen in his surname, moved first to Devon to play the part of a country squire, and then to France to a life of seclusion. Shaw thought that he had buried himself alive and could never reconcile himself to the loss. It was, as his biographer

Hesketh Pearson said: 'The only important matter about which he asked me to be reticent.'

After directing many of Shaw's plays for many years, acting many of his best roles (written by Shaw with Barker in mind), dreaming and planning together the birth of a National Theatre, not to mention writing, directing, and acting in his own plays while managing his own company at the Royal Court, Barker withdrew from the theatre, and for twenty years there was silence between the two men. Only on the occasion of the death of Shaw's wife did they communicate by letters. 'I did not know I could be so moved by anything,' wrote Shaw to him.

Out of this self-exile came one major work, slowly assembled over many years: *The Prefaces to Shakespeare*. With a few exceptions (Auden on *Othello*, Barbara Everett on *Hamlet*, Jan Kott on *The Tempest*) it's the only critical work about Shakespeare that's made any impact on me, apart, that is, from my father's view of Shakespeare, which was brief and brutal: 'It's absolute balls.'

As much as we need a good father, we need a good teacher. Mine, improbably perhaps, was Kingsley Amis. He'd arrived, somewhat diffidently, at Cambridge at the same time as I did. The depth of my ignorance of English literature corresponded almost exactly to his dislike of the theatre. Nevertheless, he made me see Shakespeare with a mind uncontaminated by the views of academics, whom he would never have described as his fellows and whose views he regarded as, well, academic. I would write essays marinated in the opinions of Spurgeon, Wilson Knight, Dover Wilson and a large cast of critical supernumeraries. He would gently, but courteously, cast aside my essay about, say, *Twelfth Night*: 'But what do *you* think of this play? Do you think it's any good?' 'Well ... er ... it's Shakespeare.' 'Yes, but is it any *good*? I mean as a *play*. It says it's a comedy. Fine. But does it have any decent jokes?'

I took this for irreverence, heresy even. Over the years, however, I've come to regard this as good teaching, or, closely allied, good direction. It's asking the right questions, unintimidated by reputation, by tradition, by received opinion, or by critical orthodoxy. This was shocking, but healthy, for a young and impressionable man ripe to become a fundamentalist in matters of literary taste and ready to revere F. R. Leavis as the Ayatollah of 'Cambridge English'. What you have is yourself and the text, only that. That's the lesson of Granville Barker: 'We have the text to guide us, half a dozen stage directions, and that is all. I abide by the text and the demands of the text and beyond that I claim freedom.' I can't imagine a more useful and more enduring dictum.

The Prefaces have a practical aim: 'I want to see Shakespeare made fully effective on the English stage. That is the best sort of help I can lend.' What Granville Barker wrote is a primer for directors and actors working on the plays of Shakespeare. There is lamentably little useful literature about the making of theatre, even though there is an indigestible glut of memoirs and biographies, largely concerned with events that have taken place *after* the curtain has fallen. If I was asked by a visiting Martian to recommend books which would help him, her or it to make theatre in the manner of the European I could only offer four books: Stanislavsky on *The Art of the Stage*, John Willett's *Brecht on Theatre*, Peter Brook's *The Empty Space*, and *The Prefaces to Shakespeare*.

Stanislavsky offers a pseudo-scientific dissection of the art of acting which is, in some respects, like reading Freud on the mechanism of the joke: earnest, well-meaning, but devoid of the indispensable ingredient of its subject matter: humour. Stanislavsky's great contribution was to demand that actors hold the mirror up to nature, that they take their craft as seriously as the writers they served, and to provide some sort of formal discipline within which both aims could be realised.

Brecht provided a manifesto that was a political and aesthetic response to the baroque encrustations of the scenery-laden, star-dominated, archaic boulevard theatre of Germany in the twenties. Although much of what he wrote as theory is an unpalatable mix of political ideology and artistic instruction, it is his theatrical instinct that prevails. He asserts, he insists, he browbeats. He demands that the stage, like society, must be re-examined, reformed, that the audience's habits mustn't be satisfied, they must be changed, but just when he is about to nail his 13 Articles to the church door he drops the voice of the zealot: 'The stage is not a hothouse or a zoological museum full of stuffed animals. It must be peopled with live, three-dimensional self-contradictory people with their passions, unconsidered utterances and actions.' In all art forms, he says, the guardians of orthodoxy will assert that there are eternal and immutable laws that you ignore at your peril, but in the theatre there is only one inflexible rule: 'The proof of the pudding is in the eating.' Brecht teaches us to ask the question: what goes on in a theatre?

Brook takes that question even further: what *is* theatre? It's a philosophical, but eminently practical, question that Brook has been asking for over 30 years and which has taken him to the African desert, a quarry in Iran, and an abandoned music hall in Paris. 'I take an empty space and call it a bare stage. A man walks across this empty space while someone else is watching him, and that is all that is needed for an act of theatre to be engaged.' For all his apparent concern with metaphyics, there is no more practical man of the theatre than Brook.

I was once at a seminar where someone asked him what was the job of the director. 'To get the actors on and off stage,' he said. Like Brecht, like Stanislavsky, like Granville Barker, Brook argues that for the theatre to be expressive it must be, above all, simple and unaffected: a distillation of language, of gesture, of action, of design, where meaning is the essence. The meaning must be felt as much as understood. 'They don't have to understand with their ears,' says Granville Barker, 'just with their guts.'

Brecht did not acknowledge a debt to Granville Barker. Perhaps he was not aware of one, but it seems to me that Barker's Shakespeare productions were the direct antecedents of Brecht's work. He certainly knew enough about English theatre to know that he was on to a good thing adapting *The Beggar's Opera*, *The Recruiting Officer* and *Coriolanus*. Brecht has been lauded for destroying illusionism; Granville Barker has been unhymned. He aimed at re-establishing the relationship between actor and audience that had existed in Shakespeare's theatre – and this at a time when the prevailing style of Shakespearean production involved *not* stopping short of having live sheep in *As You Like It*. He abolished footlights and the proscenium arch, building out an apron over the orchestra pit which Shaw said 'apparently trebled the spaciousness of the stage. . . . To the imagination it looks as if he had invented a new heaven and a new earth.'

His response to staging Shakespeare was not to look for a synthetic Elizabethanism. 'We shall not save our souls by being Elizabethan.' To recreate the Globe would, he knew, be aesthetic anasthaesia, involving the audience in an insincere conspiracy to pretend that they were willing collaborators in a vain effort to turn the clock back. His answers to staging Shakespeare were similar to Brecht's for *his* plays and, in some senses, to

Chekhov's for his. He wanted scenery not to decorate and be literal, but to be expressive and metaphorical, and at the same time, in apparent contradiction, to be specific and be real, while being minimal and iconographic: the cart in *Mother Courage*, the nursery in *The Cherry Orchard*, the dining table in *The Voysey Inheritance*. 'To create a new hieroglyphic language of scenery. That, in a phrase, is the problem. If the designer finds himself competing with the actors, the sole interpreters Shakespeare has licensed, then it is he that is the intruder and must retire.'

In *The Prefaces* Granville Barker argues for a fluency of staging unbroken by scene changes. Likewise the verse should be spoken fast. 'Be swift, be swift, be not poetical,' he wrote on the dressing-room mirror of Cathleen Nesbitt when she played Perdita. Within the speed, however, detailed reality. *Meaning* above all.

It is the director's task, with the actors, to illuminate the meanings of a play: its vocabulary, its syntax, and its philosophy. The director has to ask what each scene is revealing about the characters and their actions: what story is each scene telling us? In *The Prefaces* Granville Barker exhumes, examines and explains the lost stagecraft of Shakespeare line by line, scene by scene, play by play.

Directing Shakespeare is a matter of understanding the meaning of a scene and staging it in the light of that knowledge. Easier said than done, but it's at the heart of the business of directing any play, and directing Shakespeare is merely directing writ large. Beyond that, as David Mamet has observed, 'choice of actions and adverbs constitute the craft of directing'. Get up from that chair and walk across the room. Slowly.

With Shakespeare as with any other playwright the director's job is to make the play live, now, in the present tense. 'Spontaneous enjoyment is the life of the theatre,' says Granville Barker in his Preface to *Love's Labour's Lost*. To receive a review, as Granville Barker did, headed *SHAKESPEARE ALIVE!* is the most, but should be the least, that a director must hope for.

I regard Granville Barker not only as the first modern English director but as the most influential. Curiously, partly as a result of his early withdrawal from the theatre, partly because his *Prefaces* have been out of print for many years, and partly because of his own self-effacement, he has been unjustly ignored both in the theatre and in the academic world, where the codification of their 'systems' has resulted in the canonisation of Brecht and Stanislavsky. I hope the re-publication of *The Prefaces* will right the balance. Granville Barker himself always thought of them as his permanent legacy to the theatre.

My sense of filial identification is not entirely a professional one. When I directed *The Voysey Inheritance* I wanted a photograph of the author on the poster. A number of people protested that it was the height, or depth, of vanity and self-aggrandisement to put my own photograph on the poster. I was astonished, I was bewildered, but I was not unflattered. I still can't see the resemblance, but it's not through lack of trying.

Two years ago the Royal National Theatre was presented with a wonderful bronze bust of Granville Barker by Katherine Scott (the wife, incidentally, of the Antarctic hero). For a while it sat on the windowsill of my office like a benign household god. Then it was installed on a bracket in the foyer opposite a bust of Olivier, the two men eyeing each other in wary mutual regard. A few months later it was stolen; an act of homage perhaps. I miss him.

Richard Eyre

Introduction

We have still much to learn about Shakespeare the playwright. Strange that it should be so, after three centuries of commentary and performance, but explicable. For the Procrustean methods of a changed theatre deformed the plays, and put the art of them to confusion; and scholars, with this much excuse, have been apt to divorce their Shakespeare from the theatre altogether, to think him a poet whose use of the stage was quite incidental, whose glory had small relation to it, for whose lapses it was to blame.

The Study and the Stage

THIS much is to be said for Garrick and his predecessors and successors in the practice of reshaping Shakespeare's work to the theatre of their time. The essence of it was living drama to them, and they meant to keep it alive for their public. They wanted to avoid whatever would provoke question and so check that spontaneity of response upon which acted drama depends. Garrick saw the plays, with their lack of 'art', through the spectacles of contemporary culture; and the bare Elizabethan stage, if it met his mind's eye at all, doubtless as a barbarous makeshift. Shakespeare was for him a problem; he tackled it, from our point of view, misguidedly and with an overplus of enthusiasm. His was a positive world; too near in time, moreover, as well as too opposed in taste to Shakespeare's to treat it perspectively. The romantic movement might have brought a more concordant outlook. But by then the scholars were off their own way; while the theatre began to think of its Shakespeare from the point of view of the picturesque, and, later, in terms of upholstery. Nineteenth-century drama developed along the lines of realistic illusion, and the staging of Shakespeare was further subdued to this, with inevitably disastrous effect on the speaking of his verse; there was less perversion of text perhaps, but actually more wrenching of the construction of the plays for the convenience of the stage carpenter. The public appetite for this sort of thing having been gorged, producers then turned to newer—and older—contrivances, leaving 'realism' (so called) to the modern comedy that had fathered it. Amid much vaporous theorizing—but let us humbly own how hard it is not to write nonsense about art, which seems ever pleading to be enjoyed and not written about at all—the surprising discovery had been made that varieties of stagecraft and stage were not historical accidents but artistic obligations, that Greek drama belonged in a Greek theatre, that Elizabethan plays, therefore, would, presumably, do best upon an Elizabethan stage, that there was nothing sacrosanct about scenery, footlights, drop-curtain or any of their belongings. This brings us to the present situation.

There are few enough Greek theatres in which Greek tragedy can be played; few enough people want to see it, and they will applaud it encouragingly however it is done. Some acknowledgement is due to the altruism of the doers! Shakespeare is another matter. The English theatre, doubtful of its destiny, of necessity venal, opening its doors to all comers, seems yet, as by some instinct, to seek renewal of strength in him. An actor, unless success has made him cynical, or his talent be merely trivial, may take some pride in the hall mark of Shakespearean achievement. So may a manager if he thinks he can afford it. The public (or their spokesmen) seem to consider Shakespeare and his genius a sort of national property, which, truly, they do nothing to conserve, but in which they have moral rights not lightly to be flouted. The production of the plays is thus still apt to be marked by a timid respect for 'the usual thing'; their acting is crippled by pseudo-traditions, which are inert because they are not Shakespearean at all. They are the accumulation of two centuries of progressive misconception and distortion of his playwright's art. On the other hand, England has been spared production of Shakespeare according to this or that even more irrelevant theory of presentationalism, symbolism, constructivism or what not. There is the breach in the wall of 'realism', but we have not yet made up our minds to pass through, taking our Shakespeare with us.

Incidentally, we owe the beginning of the breach to Mr William Poel, who, with fanatical courage, when 'realism' was at the tottering height of its triumph in the later revivals of Sir Henry Irving, and the yet more richly upholstered revelations of Sir Herbert Tree, thrust the Elizabethan stage in all its apparent eccentricity upon our unwilling notice.[1] Mr Poel shook complacency. He could not expect to do much more; for he was a logical reformer. He showed us the Elizabethan stage, with Antony and Cleopatra, Troilus and Cressida, in their ruffs and farthingales as for Shakespeare's audiences they lived. Q.E.D. There, however, as far as the popular theatre was concerned, the matter seemed to rest for twenty years or so. But it was just such a demonstration that was needed; anything less drastic and provocative might have been passed over with mild approval.

To get the balance true, let us admit that while Shakespeare was an Elizabethan playwright he was—and now is to us—predominantly something much more. Therefore we had better not too unquestioningly thrust him back within the confines his genius has escaped, nor presume him to have felt the pettier circumstances of his theatre sacrosanct. Nor can we turn Elizabethans as we watch the plays; and every mental effort to do so will subtract from our enjoyment of them. This is the case against the circumstantial reproduction of Shakespeare's staging. But Mr Poel's achievement remains; he cleared for us from Shakespeare's stagecraft the scenic rubbish by which it had been so long encumbered and disguised. And we could now, if we would, make a promising fresh start. For the scholars, on their side, have lately—the scholarly among them—cut clear of the transcendental fog (scenic illusion of another sort) in which their nineteenth-century peers loved to lose themselves, and they too are beginning again at the beginning. A text acquires virtue now by its claim to be a prompt book, and the most comprehensive work of our time upon the Elizabethan stage is an elaborate sorting-out of plays, companies and theatres. On Dr Pollard's treatment of the texts and on the foundations of fact laid by Sir Edmund Chambers a new scholarship is rising, aiming first to see Shakespeare in the theatre for which he wrote. It is a scholarship, therefore, by which the theatre of today can profit, to which, by its acting of Shakespeare, it could contribute, one would hope. Nor should the scholars disdain the help; for criticism cannot live upon criticism, it needs refreshment from the living art. Besides, what is all the criticism and scholarship finally for if not to keep Shakespeare alive? And he must always be most alive—even if roughly and rudely alive—in the theatre. Let the scholars force a way in there, if need be. Its fervid atmosphere will do them good; the benefit will be mutual.

These Prefaces are an attempt to profit by this new scholarship and to contribute to it some research into Shakespeare's stagecraft, by examining the plays, one

after another, in the light of the interpretation he designed for them, so far as this can be deduced; to discover,
if possible, the production he would have desired for
them, all merely incidental circumstances apart. They
might profit more written a generation hence, for the
ground they build upon is still far from clear. And this
introduction is by no means a conspectus of the subject;
that can only come as a sequel. There has been, in this
branch of Shakespearean study, too much generalization
and far too little analysis of material.[2]

Shakespeare's Stagecraft

SHAKESPEARE'S own career was not a long one. The
whole history of the theatre he wrote for does not cover
a century. Between Marlowe and Massinger, from the
first blaze to the glowing of the embers, it is but fifty
years. Yet even while Shakespeare was at work, the stage
to which he fitted his plays underwent constant and
perhaps radical change. From Burbage's first theatre to
the Globe, then to Blackfriars, not to mention excursions
to Court and into the great halls—change of audiences
and their behaviour, of their taste, development of the
art of acting, change of the stage itself and its resources
were all involved in the progress, and are all, we may
be sure, reflected to some degree in the plays themselves.
We guess at the conditions of each sort of stage and
theatre, but there is often the teasing question to which
of them had a play, as we have it now, been adapted.
And of the 'private' theatre, most in vogue for the ten
years preceding the printing of the First Folio so far we
know least. The dating of texts and their ascription to
the usages of a particular theatre may often be a search-
light upon their stagecraft. Here is much work for the
new scholarship.

Conversely, the watchful working-out of the plays in action upon this stage or that would be of use to the scholars, who otherwise must reconstruct their theatre and gloss their texts as in a vacuum. The play was once fitted to the stage; it is by no means impossible to rebuild that stage now, with its doors, balconies, curtains and machines, by measuring the needs of the play. It is idle, for instance, to imagine scenes upon inner or upper stage without evidence that they will be audible or visible there; and editing is still vitiated by lack of this simple knowledge. Here, if nowhere else, this present research must fall short, for its method should rightly be experimental; more than one mind should be at work on it, moreover.

The text of a play is a score waiting performance, and the performance and its preparation are, almost from the beginning, a work of collaboration. A producer may direct the preparation, certainly. But if he only knows how to give orders, he has mistaken his vocation; he had better be a drill-sergeant. He might talk to his company when they all met together for the first time to study *Love's Labour's Lost*, *Julius Cæsar* or *King Lear*, on some such lines as these Prefaces pursue, giving a considered opinion of the play, drawing a picture of it in action, providing, in fact, a hypothesis which mutual study would prove—and might partly disprove. No sort of study of a play can better the preparation of its performance if this is rightly done. The matured art of the playwright lies in giving life to characters in action, and the secret of it in giving each character a due chance in the battle, the action of a play becoming literally the fighting of a battle of character. So the greater the playwright, the wider and deeper his sympathies, the more genuine this opposition will be and the less easily will a single mind grasp it, as it must be grasped, in the fullness of its emotion. The dialogue of a play runs—and often intricately—upon lines of reason, but it is charged besides with an emotion which speech releases, yet only releases fully when the speaker is—as an actor is—identified with the character. There is further the incidental action, implicit in the dialogue, which springs to life only when a scene is in being. A play, in fact, as we find it written, is a magic spell; and even the magician cannot always foresee the full effect of it.

Not every play, it must be owned, will respond to such intensive study. Many, ambitiously conceived, would collapse under the strain. Many are mere occasions for display of their actors' wit or eloquence, good looks or nice behaviour, and meant to be no more; and if they are skilfully contrived the parts fit together and the whole machine should go like clockwork. Nor, in fact, are even the greatest plays often so studied. There is hardly a theatre in the world where masterpiece and trumpery alike are not rushed through rehearsals to an arbitrarily effective performance, little more learned of them than the words, gaps in the understanding of them filled up with 'business'—effect without cause, the demand for this being the curse of the theatre as of other arts, as of other things than art. Not to such treatment will the greater plays of Shakespeare yield their secrets. But working upon a stage which reproduced the essential conditions of his, working as students, not as showmen merely, a company of actors might well find many of the riddles of the library answering themselves unasked. And these Prefaces could best be a record of such work, if such work were to be done.

We cannot, on the other hand, begin our research by postulating the principles of the Elizabethan stage. One is tempted to say it had none, was too much a child of nature to bother about such things. Principles were doubtless imposed upon it when it reached respectability, and heads would be bowed to the yoke. Shakespeare's among them? He had served a most practical apprenticeship to his trade. If he did not hold horses at the door, he sat behind the curtains, we may be sure, and held the prompt book on occasion. He acted, he cobbled other men's plays, he could write his own to order. Such a one may stay a journeyman if he is not a genius, but he will not become a doctrinaire. Shakespeare's work shows such principles as the growth of a tree shows. It is not haphazard merely because it is not formal; it is shaped by inner strength. The theatre, as he found it, allowed him and encouraged him to great freedom of development. Because the material resources of a stage are simple, it does not follow that the technique of its playwriting will stay so. Crude work may show up more crudely, when there are none of the fal-lals of illusion to disguise it that the modern theatre provides. But, if he has it in him, a dramatist can, so unfettered, develop the essentials of his art more boldly and more subtly too. The Elizabethan drama made an amazingly quick advance from crudity to an excellence which was often technically most elaborate. The advance and the not less amazing gulf which divides its best from its worst may be ascribed to the simplicity of the machinery it employed. That its decadence was precipitated by the influence of the Masque and the shifting of its centre of interest from the barer public stage to the candle-lit private theatre, where the machinery of the Masque became effective, it would be rash to assert; but the occurrences are suspiciously related. Man and machine (here at any rate is a postulate, if a platitude!) are false allies in the theatre, secretly at odds; and when man gets the worst of it, drama is impoverished; and the struggle, we may add, is perennial. No great drama depends upon pageantry. All great drama tends to concentrate upon character; and, even so, not upon picturing men as they show themselves to the world like figures on a stage— though that is how it must ostensibly show them—but on the hidden man. And the progress of Shakespeare's art from *Love's Labour's Lost* to *Hamlet*, and thereafter with a difference, lies in the simplifying of this paradox and the solving of the problem it presents; and the process involves the developing of a very subtle sort of stagecraft indeed.

For one result we have what we may call a very self-contained drama. Its chief values, as we know, have not changed with the fashions of the theatre. It relies much on the music of the spoken word, and a company of schoolchildren with pleasant voices, and an ear for rhythm, may vociferate through a play to some effect. It is as much to be enjoyed in the reading, if we hear it in imagination as we read, as drama meant to be acted can be. As with its simplicities then, so it should be, we presume, with its complexities. The subtly emotional use of verse and the interplay of motive and character, can these not be appreciated apart from the bare boards of their original setting? It does not follow. It neither follows that the advantages of the Elizabethan stage were wholly negative nor that, with our present knowledge, we can imagine the full effect of a play in action upon it. The imagining of a play in action is, under no circumstances, an easy thing.[3] What would one not give to go backward through the centuries to see the first performance of *Hamlet*, played as Shakespeare had it played![4] In default, if we could but make ourselves read it as if it were a manuscript fresh from its author's hands! There is much to be said for turning one's back on the editors, even, when possible, upon the First Folio with its demarcation of acts and scenes, in favour of the Quartos—Dr Pollard's 'good' Quartos—in their yet greater simplicity.

The Convention of Place

IT is, for instance, hard to discount the impression made merely by reading: *Scene i—Elsinore. A platform before the Castle*; and most of us have, to boot, early memories of painted battlements and tenth-century castles (of ageing Hamlets and their portly mothers for that matter) very difficult to dismiss. No great harm, one protests; it was a help, perhaps, to the unimaginative. But it is a first step to the certain misunderstanding of Shakespeare's stagecraft. The 'if, how and when' of the presenting of localities on the Elizabethan stage is, of course, a complex question. Shakespeare himself seems to have followed, consciously, no principles in the matter, nor was his practice very logical, nor at all consistent. It may vary with the play he is writing and the particular stage he is writing for; it will best be studied in relation to each play. We can, however, free ourselves from one general misconception which belongs to our own over-logical standpoint. When we learn with a shock of surprise—having begun in the schoolroom upon the Shakespeare of the editors, it comes as belated news to us—that neither battlements, throne rooms nor picturesque churchyards were to be seen at the Globe, and that *Elsinore. A platform before the Castle* is not Shakespeare at all, we yet imagine ourselves among the audience there busily conjuring these things up before the eye of faith. The Elizabethan audience was at no such pains. Nor was this their alternative to seeing the actors undisguisedly concerned with the doors, curtains and balconies which, by the play's requirements, should have been anything but what they were. As we, when a play has no hold on us, may fall to thinking about the scenery, so to a Globe audience, unmoved, the stage might be an obvious bare stage. But are we conscious of the scenery behind the actor when the play really moves us? If we are, there is something very wrong with the scenery, which should know its place as a background. The audience was not conscious of curtain and balcony when Burbage played Hamlet to them. They were conscious of Hamlet. That conventional background faded as does our painted illusion, and they certainly did not deliberately conjure up in its place mental pictures of Elsinore. The genus audience is passive, if expectant, imaginatively lazy till roused, never, one may be sure, at pains to make any effort that is generally unnecessary to enjoyment.

With Shakespeare the locality of a scene has dramatic importance, or it has none; and this is as true of his early plays as his late ones. Both in *Richard II* and *Antony and Cleopatra*, scene after scene passes with no exact indication of where we may be. With *Cleopatra* we are surely in Egypt, with Cæsar in Rome. Pompey appears, and the talk tells us that both Egypt and Rome are elsewhere; but positively where Pompey is at the moment we never learn.[5] Indoors or outdoors? The action of the scene or the clothing of the characters will tell us this if we need to know. But, suddenly transported to the Parthian war, our whereabouts is made amply plain. It is, however, made plain by allusion. The information peeps out through talk of kindred things; we are hardly aware we are being told, and, again, we learn no more than we need to learn. This, truly, is a striking development from the plump and plain

> Barkloughly Castle call they this at hand?

of Richard II, even from the more descriptive

> I am a stranger here in Gloucestershire:
> These high wild hills and rough, uneven ways
> Draw out our miles. . .

by which Shakespeare pictures and localizes the manoeuvres of Richard and Bolingbroke when he wants to.
But the purpose is the same, and the method essentially
the same.[6] Towards the end of the later play come scene
after scene of the marching and countermarching of
armies, of fighting, of truce, all the happenings of three
days' battle. Acts III and IV contain twenty-eight scenes
long and short; some of them are very short; three of
them have but four lines apiece. The editors conscientiously ticket them *A plain near Actium, Another part of the
plain, Another part of the plain* and so on, and conclude that
Shakespeare is really going too far and too fast, is indeed
(I quote Sir Edmund Chambers) 'in some danger of
outrunning the apprehensions of his auditory.' Indeed he
might be if this cinematographic view of his intentions
were the right one! But it utterly falsifies them. Show an
audience such a succession of painted scenes—if you
could at the pace required—and they would give attention to nothing else whatever; the drama would pass
unnoticed. Had Shakespeare tried to define the whereabouts of every scene in any but the baldest phrases—the
protesting editors seem not to see that he makes no
attempt to; only *they* do!—he would have had to lengthen
and complicate them; had he written only a labelling
line or two he would still have distracted his audience
from the essential drama. Ignoring whereabouts, letting
it at most transpire when it naturally will, the characters
capture all attention. This is the true gain of the bare
stage; unless to some dramatic end no precious words
need be spent, in complying with the undramatic demands of space and time; incarnation of character can
be all in all. Given such a crisis as this the gain is yet
greater. We are carried through the phases of the three
days' battle; and what other stage convention would
allow us so varied a view of it, could so isolate the true

drama of it? For do we not pass through such a crisis in reality with just that indifference to time and place? These scenes, in their kind, show Shakespeare's stage-craft, not at its most reckless, but at its very best, and exemplify perfectly the freedom he enjoyed that the stage of visual illusion has inevitably lost. His drama is attached solely to its actors and their acting; that, perhaps, puts it in a phrase. They carry place and time with them as they move. The modern theatre still accepts the convention that measures time more or less by a play's convenience; a half-hour stands for an hour or more, and we never question the vagary. It was no more strange to an Elizabethan audience to see a street in Rome turned, in the use made of it, to the Senate House by the drawing of a curtain and the disclosure of Cæsar's state, to find Cleopatra's Monument now on the upper stage because Antony had to be drawn up to it, later on the lower because Cleopatra's death-scene could best be played there; it would seem that they were not too astonished even when Juliet, having taken leave of Romeo on the balcony of her bedroom and watched him descend to the lower stage, the scene continuing, came down, a few lines later, to the lower stage herself, bringing, so to speak, her bedroom with her—since this apparently is what she must have done.[7] For neither Senate House, Monument nor balcony had rights and reality of their own. They existed for the convenience of the actors, whose touch gave them life, a shadowy life at most; neglected, they existed no longer.[8]

Shakespeare's stagecraft concentrates, and inevitably, upon opportunity for the actor. We think now of the plays themselves; their first public knew them by their acting; and the development of the actor's art from the agilities and funniments of the clown, and from round-mouthed rhetoric to imaginative interpreting of character by such standards as Hamlet set up for his players, was a factor in the drama's triumph that we now too often ignore. Shakespeare himself, intent more and more upon plucking out the heart of the human mystery, stimulated his actors to a poignancy and intimacy of emotional expression—still can stimulate them to it—as no other playwright has quite learned to do.

The Speaking of the Verse

His verse was, of course, his chief means to this emotional expression; and when it comes to staging the plays, the speaking of verse must be the foundation of all study. The changes of three hundred years have of themselves put difficulties in our way here; though there are some besides—as one imagines—of Shakespeare's own making. Surely his syntax must now and then have puzzled even his contemporaries. Could they have made much more than we can of Leontes'

> Affection! thy intention stabs the centre;
> Thou dost make possible things not so held,
> Communicat'st with dreams;—How can this be?
> With what's unreal thou coactive art,
> And fellow'st nothing; then, 'tis very credent
> Thou may'st co-join with something; and thou dost;
> And that beyond commission; and I find it,
> And that to the infection of my brains,
> And hardening of my brows.

The confusion of thought and intricacy of language is dramatically justified. Shakespeare is picturing a genuinely jealous man (the sort of man that Othello was *not*) in the grip of a mental epilepsy. We parse the passage and dispute its sense; spoken, as it was meant to be, in a choking torrent of passion, probably a modicum of sense slipped through, and its first hearers did not find it a mere rigmarole. But we are apt to miss even that much. Other passages, of early and late writing, may always have had as much sound as sense to them; but now, to the casual hearer, they will convey more sound than sense by far. Nor do puns mean to us what they meant to the Elizabethans, delighting in their language for its own sake. Juliet's tragic fantasia upon 'Aye' and 'I' sounds all but ridiculous, and one sympathizes with an actress hesitating to venture on it. How far, apart from the shifting of accents and the recolouring of vowels, has not the whole habit of English speech changed in these three hundred years? In the theatre it was slowing down, one fancies, throughout the eighteenth century; and in the nineteenth, as far as Shakespeare was concerned, it grew slower and slower, till on occasions one thought—even hoped—that shortly the actor would stop altogether. There may have been more than one cause; imitation of the French Augustans, the effort to make antiquated phrases understood, the increasing size of the theatres themselves would all contribute to it. The result, in any case, is disastrous. Elizabethan drama was built upon vigour and beauty of speech. The groundlings may often have deserved Shakespeare's strictures, but they would stand in discomfort for an hour or so to be stirred by the sound of verse. Some of the actors no doubt were robustious periwigpated fellows, but, equally, it was no empty ideal of acting he put into Hamlet's mouth—and Burbage's. We may suppose that at its best the mere speaking of the plays was a very brilliant thing, compared to *bel canto*, or to a pianist's virtuosity. The emotional appeal of our modern music was in it, and it could be tested by ears trained to the rich and delicate fretwork of the music of that day. Most Hamlets—not being playwrights—make a mild joke of telling us they'd as lief the town-crier spoke their lines, but we may hear in it the echo of some of Shakespeare's sorest trials.

The speaking of his verse must be studied, of course, in relation to the verse's own development. The actor must not attack its supple complexities in *Antony and Cleopatra* and *Cymbeline*, the mysterious dynamics of *Macbeth*, the nobilities of *Othello*, its final pastoral simplicities in *A Winter's Tale* and *The Tempest* without preliminary training in the lyricism, the swift brilliance and the masculine clarity of the earlier plays. A modern actor, alas, thinks it simple enough to make his way, splay-footed, through

The cloud-capped towers, the gorgeous palaces . . .

though Berowne's

I, forsooth, in love . . .

or one of Oberon's apostrophes will defeat him utterly. And, without an ear trained to the delicacy of the earlier work, his hearers, for their part, will never know how shamefully he is betraying the superb ease of the later. If we are to make Shakespeare our own again we must all be put to a little trouble about it. We must recapture as far as may be his lost meanings; and the sense of a phrase we *can* recapture, though instinctive emotional response to it may be a loss forever. The tunes that he writes to, the whole great art of his music-making, we can master. Actors can train their ears and tongues and can train our ears to it. We talk of lost arts. No art is ever lost while the means to it survive. Our faculties rust by disuse and by misuse are coarsened, but they quickly recover delight in a beautiful thing. Here, at any rate, is the touchstone by which all interpreting of Shakespeare the playwright must first—and last—be tried.

The Boy-Actress

MORE than one of the conditions of his theatre made this medium of accomplished speech of such worth to him. Boys played the women parts; and what could a boy bring to Juliet, Rosalind or Cleopatra beyond grace of manner and charm of speech? We have been used to women on the stage for two hundred and fifty years or more, and a boy Juliet—if the name on the programme revealed one, for nothing else might—would seem an odd fish to us; no one would risk a squeaking Cleopatra; though, as for Rosalind, through three-parts of the play a boy would have the best of it. But the parts were written for boys; not, therefore, without consideration of how boys could act them most convincingly. Hence, of course, the popularity of the heroine so disguised. The disguise was perfect; the make-believe one degree more complex, certainly, than it needs to be with us; but once you start make-believe it matters little how far you go with it; there is, indeed, some enjoyment in the make-believe itself. But, further, it is Shakespeare's constant care to demand nothing of a boy-actress that might turn to unseemliness or ridicule. He had not much taste for what is called 'domestic drama,' nor does he dose us very heavily with Doll Tearsheet, Mistress Overdone and their like. Constance mourns Arthur's loss, Lady Macduff has her little son, but no mother croons over the child in her arms. Paulina brings Hermione's baby to Leontes, it is true; but see with what tact, from this point of view, the episode is managed. And love-scenes are most carefully contrived. Romeo and Juliet are seldom alone together; never for long, but in the balcony-scene; and in this, the most famous of love-scenes, they are kept from all contact with each other. Consider *Antony and*

Cleopatra. Here is a tragedy of sex without one single scene of sexual appeal. That aspect of Cleopatra is reflected for us in talk about her; mainly by Enobarbus, who is not mealymouthed; but his famed description of her voluptuousness is given us when she has been out of our sight for several scenes. The play opens with her parting from Antony, and in their two short encounters we see her swaying him by wit, malice and with the moods of her mind. Not till the story takes its tragic plunge and sex is drowned in deeper passion are they ever intimately together; till he is brought to her dying there has been occasion for but one embrace. Contrast this with a possible Cleopatra planned to the advantage of the actress of today.

Shakespeare, artist that he was, turned this limitation to account, made loss into a gain.[9] Feminine charm—of which the modern stage makes such capital—was a medium denied him. So his men and women encounter upon a plane where their relation is made rarer and intenser by poetry, or enfranchised in a humour which surpasses more primitive love-making. And thus, perhaps, he was helped to discover that the true stuff of tragedy and of the liveliest comedy lies beyond sensual bounds. His studies of women seem often to be begun from some spiritual paces beyond the point at which a modern dramatist leaves off. Curious that not a little of the praise lavished upon the beauty and truth of them—mainly by women—may be due to their having been written to be played by boys!

Much could be said for the restoring of the celibate stage; but the argument, one fears, would be academic. Here, though, is practical counsel. Let the usurping actress remember that her sex is a liability, not an asset. The dramatist of today may refuse to exploit its allurements, but may legitimately allow for the sympathetic effect of it; though the less he does so, perhaps, the better for his play and the more gratitude the better sort of actress will show him. But Shakespeare makes no such demands, has left no blank spaces for her to fill with her charm. He asks instead for self-forgetful clarity of perception, and for a sensitive, spirited, athletic beauty of speech and conduct, which will leave prettiness and its lures at a loss, and the crudities of more Circean appeal looking very crude indeed.

The Soliloquy

THIS convention of the boy-actress may be said to give a certain remoteness to a play's acting. The soliloquy brings a compensating intimacy, and its use was an important part of Shakespeare's stagecraft. Its recognized usefulness was for the disclosing of the plot, but he soon improved upon this. Soliloquy becomes the means by which he brings us not only to a knowledge of the more secret thoughts of his characters, but into the closest emotional touch with them too. Here the platform stage helped him, as the stage of scenic illusion now defeats his purpose. But it is not altogether a question of 'realism' and the supposed obligation this lays upon a real man in a real-looking room to do nothing he would not do if the whole affair were real.

There is no escape from convention in the theatre, and all conventions can be made acceptable, though they cannot all be used indiscriminately, for they are founded in the physical conditions of the stage of their origin and are often interdependent one with another. Together they form a code, and they are as a treaty made with the audience. No article of it is to be abrogated unless we can be persuaded to consent, and upon its basis we surrender our imaginations to the playwright.

With the soliloquy upon the platform stage it is a case—as so often where convention is concerned—of extremes meeting. There is no illusion, so there is every illusion. Nothing very strange about this man, not even the dress he wears, leaning forward a little we could touch him; we are as intimate and familiar with him as it is possible to be. We agree to call him 'Hamlet', to suppose that he is where he says he is, we admit that he thinks aloud and in blank verse too. It is possible that the more we are asked to imagine the easier we find it to do. It is certain that, once our imagination is working, visual illusion will count for little in the stimulating of emotion beside this intimacy that allows the magnetism of personality full play.

There is no more important task for the producer of Shakespeare than to restore to the soliloquy its rightful place in a play's economy, and in particular to regain for it full emotional effect. We now accept the convention frigidly, the actor manoeuvres with it timidly. Banished behind footlights into that other world of illusion, the solitary self-communing figure rouses our curiosity at best. Yet further adapted to the self-contained methods of modern acting, the soliloquy has quite inevitably become a slack link in the play's action, when it should be a recurring reinforcement to its strength. Shakespeare never pinned so many dramatic fortunes to a merely utilitarian device. Time and again he may be feeling his way through a scene for a grip on his audience, and it is the soliloquy ending it that will give him—and his actor—the stranglehold. When he wishes to quicken the pulse of the action, to screw up its tension in a second or so, the soliloquy serves him well. For a parallel to its full effectiveness on Shakespeare's stage we should really look to the modern music-hall comedian getting on terms with his audience. We may measure the response to Burbage's

O, that this too too solid flesh would melt . . .

by recalling—those of us that happily can—Dan Leno
as a washerwoman, confiding domestic troubles to a
theatre full of friends, and taken unhindered to their
hearts. The problem is not really a difficult one. If we
solve the physical side of it by restoring, in essentials,
the relation between actor and audience that the intimacy of the platform stage provided, the rest should soon
solve itself.

Costume

THE problem of costume, when it arises, is a subtler one;
nor probably is it capable of any logical solution. Half
the plays can be quite appropriately dressed in the
costume of Shakespeare's own time. It is a false logic
which suggests that to match their first staging we should
dress them in the costume of ours. For with costume
goes custom and manners—or the lack of them. It may
be both a purge and a tonic to the sluggish-fancied
spectator to be shown a Prince of Denmark in coat and
trousers and a Grave-digger in a bowler hat, for remin-
der that here is a play, not a collection of ritualized
quotations. But physic is for the sick; also, there may be
less drastic cures. When archaeology took hold upon the
nineteenth-century mind it became a matter of moment
to lodge Hamlet in historic surroundings; and withers
were wrung by the anachronisms of ducats and a murder
of Gonzago, French rapiers and the rest. A needlessly
teasing difficulty; why reproduce it in terms of a young
man in a dinner jacket searching for a sword—a thing
not likely to be lying about in his modern mother's sitting
room—with which to kill Polonius, who certainly has
window curtains to hide behind instead of arras? This

gain of intimacy—with a Hamlet we might find sitting opposite at a dinner party—may well be a gain in sympathy. It was originally a great gain, a gift to Shakespeare's audience. But we pay too high a price for it.

What was the actual Elizabethan practice in this matter of costuming is not comprehensively known. We can only say safely that, as with other matters, it was neither constant, consistent, nor, from our present point of view, rational. It was based upon the use of the clothes of the time; but these might be freely and fantastically adapted to suit a particular play or advantage some character in it. Dramatic effect was probably the first consideration and the last. There were such fancy dresses as Oberon or Puck or Caliban might wear; there was always the symbolizing of royalty, and a king would wear a crown whenever he could; there was the utility of knowing Romans from Britons by sight in *Cymbeline*, the martial Roman from the effete Egyptian in *Antony and Cleopatra*, and a Scottish lord when you saw him in *Macbeth*, if we may judge by Malcolm's comment upon Rosse's appearance:

My countryman; and yet I know him not.

Our difficulty, of course, arises mainly over the historical plays. Not over the English Histories, even so; we can dress Richard III or Henry V by the light of our own superior knowledge of what they wore, and never find it clash violently with anything Shakespeare has put on their backs or in their mouths. But when we come to Julius Cæsar plucking open his doublet, to the conspirators against him with their hats about their ears, and to Cleopatra's

Cut my lace, Charmian.

not to mention British Imogen in her doublet and hose, we must stop and consider.

The common practice is, in these instances, to ignore the details of Shakespeare's text altogether; to dress Cæsar in his toga, Cleopatra in her habit as she lived, with never a stay-lace about her (though, truly, the costumier, let alone, will tend to get his fashion a few thousand years wrong and turn her out more like the wife of Tutankhamen); and as to Imogen and her surroundings, we do our best to compromise with skins and woad. This may be a lesser evil than presenting a Cæsar recalling Sir Walter Raleigh and a Cleopatra who would make us think of Mary Queen of Scots, but it is no solution of the problem. For the actors have to speak these lines, and if action and appearance contradict them, credibility is destroyed. And the constant credibility of the actor must be a producer's first care. Nor is this all, nor is it, perhaps, the most important thing to consider. The plays are full of reference, direct and indirect, to Elizabethan custom. They are, further, impregnated with what we call 'Renaissance feeling', some more, some less, but all to a degree. Now of this last we have a sense which is likelier to be a better help to their appreciation than any newfangled knowledge of the correct cut of Cleopatra's clothes will be! We know Iago for a Machiavellian figure (so called), and miss none of Shakespeare's intention. But if ever two men breathed the air of a sixteenth-century court, Hamlet and Claudius of Denmark do, and to relate them in habit and behaviour to the twilight figures of Saxo Grammaticus is as much a misinterpretation as any mauling of the text can be. They exist essentially doubtless—as do all the major characters of the plays—in their perennial humanity. But never let us forget the means by which this deeper truth of them is made vivid and actual. There have been better intellects than Shakespeare's, and poetry as good as his. He holds his supreme place by his dramatist's necessary power of bringing thought and vague emotion to the terms of action and convincing speech; further, and far more than is often allowed, by his peculiar gift of bringing into contribution the common-place traffic of life. However wide the spoken word may range, there must be the actor, anchored to the stage. However high, then, with Shakespeare, the thought or emotion may soar, we shall always find the transcendental set in the familiar. He keeps this balance constantly adjusted; and, at his play's greatest moments, when he must make most sure of our response, he will employ the simplest means. The higher arguments of the plays are thus kept always within range, and their rooted humanity blossoms in a fertile upspringing of expressive little things. Neglect or misinterpret these, the inner wealth of Shakespeare will remain, no doubt, and we may mine for it, but we shall have levelled his landscape bare.

Shakespeare's own attitude in this matter of costume and customs was as inconsistent as his practice was casual. He knew what *his* Cæsar or Cleopatra would be wearing and would casually drop in a reference to it. Yet the great Romans themselves were aliens to him. The great idea of Rome fired his imagination. Brutus, Cassius and Antony do not turn typical Elizabethan gentlemen; and to the end of that play he is striving to translate Plutarch. Whenever, on the other hand, even for a moment he has made a character all his own, he cannot but clothe it in lively familiar detail. Cleopatra's are the coquetries of a great lady of his own time, in their phrasing, in the savour. When the heights of the tragedy have to be scaled, manners will not so much matter. But if we make her, at the play's beginning, a pseudo-classic, languishing Oriental, we must do it in spite of Shakespeare, not by his help. What then is the solution of this problem, if the sight of the serpent of old Nile in a farthingale will too dreadfully offend us? We can compromise. Look at Tintoretto's and Paolo Veronese's paintings of 'classic' subjects. We accept them readily enough.

Sometimes, within the boundaries of a play, the centuries seem all at odds. *Cymbeline* need not trouble us, its Roman Britain is pure 'once upon a time'. But in *King Lear*, for instance, Shakespeare is at unwonted pains to throw us back into some heathen past. Yet Edmund is another Iago, Edgar might have been at Wittenberg with Hamlet, and Oswald steps straight from the seventeenth-century London streets. Here, though, the dominant barbarism is the important thing; the setting for Goneril and Regan, Lear's tyranny and madness, and Gloucester's blinding. To a seventeenth-century audience Oswald was so identifiable a figure that it would not matter greatly how he dressed; the modern designer of costume must show him up as best he may. Each play, in fine, if it presents a problem at all, presents its own.

The Integrity of the Text

THE text, one says at first blush, can present no problem at all. The plays should be acted as Shakespeare wrote them—how dispute it? They should be; and it is as well, before we discuss hard cases, to have the principle freely admitted. Lip service enough is done it nowadays, and Colley Cibber's *Richard III*, Tate's *Lear* and Garrick's improvements are at the back of our bookshelves, but we still find Messrs John Doe and Richard Roe slicing out lines by the dozen and even a scene or so, or chopping and changing them to suit their scenery. This will not do. Shakespeare was not a perfect playwright; there can be no such thing. Nor did he aim at a mechanical perfection, but a vitality, and this he achieved. At best then, we cut and carve the body of a play to its peril. It may be robustly, but it may be very delicately organized. And we still know little enough of the laws of its existence, and some of us, perhaps, are not such very skilful surgeons; nor is any surgeon to be recommended who operates for his own convenience.

This good rule laid down, what are the exceptions that go to prove it? There is the pornographic difficulty. This is not such a stumbling block to us as it was to Bowdler, to some bright young eyes nowadays it is quite imperceptible, in fact. Yet, saving their presence, it exists; for it exists aesthetically. Shakespeare's characters often make obscene jokes. The manners of his time permitted it. The public manners of ours still do not. Now the dramatic value of a joke is to be measured by its effect upon an audience, and each is meant to make its own sort of effect. If then, instead of giving them a passing moment's amusement, it makes a thousand people uncomfortable and for the next five minutes very self-conscious, it fails of its true effect. This argument must not be stretched to cover the silliness of turning 'God' into 'Heaven' and of making Othello call Desdemona a 'wanton' (the practice, as I recollect, of the eighteen-nineties), nor to such deodorizing of *Measure for Measure* that it becomes hard to discover what all the fuss is about. If an audience cannot think of Angelo and the Duke, Pompey and Lucio, Isabella and Mistress Overdone, and themselves to boot, as fellow-creatures all, the play is not for them. Othello must call Desdemona a 'whore', and let those that do not like it leave the theatre; what have such queasy minds to do with the pity and terror of her murder and his death? Again, to make Beatrice so mealymouthed that she may not tell us how the devil is to meet her at the gates of hell, 'like an old cuckold with horns on his head', is to dress her in a crinoline, not a farthingale. But suppression of a few of the more scabrous jokes will not leave a play much the poorer; nor, one may add, will the average playgoer be much the wiser or merrier for hearing them, since they are often quite hard to understand.

Topical passages are a similar difficulty. With their savour, if not their very meaning lost, they show like dead wood in the living tree of the dialogue and are better, one would suppose, cut away. But no hard and fast rule will apply. Macbeth's porter's farmer and equivocator will never win spontaneous laughter again. But we cannot away with them, or nothing is left of the porter. Still the baffled low comedian must not, as his wont is, obscure the lines with bibulous antics. There will be that little dead spot in the play, and nothing can be done about it. Rosencrantz' reference to the 'eyrie of children' is meaningless except to the student. Is the play the poorer for the loss of it? But the logic that will take this out had better not rob us of

> Dead shepherd, now I find thy saw of might;
> Who ever loved that loved not at first sight?

And there is the strange case of

The lady of the Strachy married the yeoman of the wardrobe.

Nobody knows what it means, but everybody finds it funny when it is spoken in its place. And this has its parallels.

In general, however, better play the plays as we find them. The blue pencil is a dangerous weapon; and its use grows on a man, for it solves too many little difficulties far too easily.

Lastly, for a golden rule, whether staging or costuming or cutting is in question, and a comprehensive creed, a producer might well pin this on his wall: Gain Shakespeare's effects by Shakespeare's means when you can; for, plainly, this will be the better way. But gain Shakespeare's effects; and it is your business to discern them.

1927

Notes

1 But it should not be forgotten that Sir Herbert Tree, happy in the orthodoxy of public favour, welcomed the heretic Mr Poel more than once to a share in his Shakespeare Festivals.

2 I do not deal in general therefore with certain vexed questions, such as act-division, which still need to be looked at, I think, in the light of the particular play.

3 I remember a most intelligent reader of a modern play missing the whole point of a scene through which the chief character was to sit conspicuously and eloquently silent. He counted only with the written dialogue. I remember, when I thought I knew *King Lear* well enough, being amazed at the effect, all dialogue apart, of the mere meeting, when I saw it, of blind Gloucester and mad Lear.

4 Though, in a sense, there was no first performance of *Hamlet*. And doubtless many of the audience for Shakespeare's new version of the old play only thought he had spoiled a good story of murder and revenge by adding too much talk to it.

5 Unless it may be said that we learn in the scene after whereabouts he *was*.

6 And in *Coriolanus*, which probably postdates *Antony and Cleopatra*, with Marcius' 'A goodly city is this Antium,' we are back to the barely informative. It serves Shakespeare's purpose; he asks no more.

7 I fancy, though, that the later Shakespeare would have thought this a clumsy device.

8 How far this is true of other dramatists than Shakespeare I do not pretend to say; nor how far, with him, the influence of the private theatre, making undoubtedly towards the scenic stage

and (much later) for illusion, did not modify his practice, when he had that stage to consider. A question, again, for the bibliographers and historians.

9   There is no evidence, of course, that he felt it a loss, no such reference to the insufficiency of the boy-actress as there is to the overself-sufficiency of the clown. Women did appear in the Masques, if only to dance, so the gulf to be bridged was not a broad one. But the Elizabethan was as shocked by the notion of women appearing upon the public stage as the Chinese playgoer is today.

A Midsummer Night's Dream (1914)

'SEPTEMBER 29th, 1662, . . . and then to the King's Theatre, where we saw *Midsummer Night's Dream*, which I had never seen before, nor shall ever again, for it is the most insipid, ridiculous play that ever I saw in my life. I saw I confess some good dancing and some handsome women, which was all my pleasure.' How many of us nowadays would dare confide that even to a cipher diary? But Pepys, as usual, is in the fashion. Shakespeare was out-moded, and the theatre manager was already bolstering up his mere poetry with sensuality and display. We have, of course, reformed all that. Still, if I must choose between this cheerful Philistine and the pious, awestruck commentator, who tells me that 'The germs of a whole philosophy of life are latent in the wayward love scenes of *A Midsummer Night's Dream*,' I turn rather to Pepys. He has done less to keep Shakespeare from his own. If you go to a theatre to scoff you may remain to enjoy yourself; if you go to pray (once in a while) you likelier leave to patronize.

Why waste time in proving that *A Midsummer Night's Dream* is a bad play, or proving otherwise, since to its deepest damnation one must add: Written by a man of a genius for the theatre, playwright in spite of himself? Does not vitality defeat doctrine? The opening of the play may be bad. The opening speech surely is even very bad dramatic verse. There is nothing much in the character of Theseus; there's nothing at all in Hippolyta. The substance of the opening scene is out of keeping

both with its own method and with the scope of the play.
But before the end of it, earlier than usual even in his
later days, Shakespeare has begun to get into his stride.
If he couldn't yet develop character he could write
poetry and—

> ... O happy fair!
> Your eyes are lode-stars; and your tongue's sweet air
> More tuneable than lark to shepherd's ear,
> When wheat is green, when hawthorn buds appear.

At the sound of that we cease to demand from Helena—for the moment at least—any more material
qualities. How he could and seemingly couldn't help but
flower into verse! It was still a question, I suppose,
whether he remained a poet or became a dramatist. He
was in every sense nearer to 'Venus and Adonis' than
Macbeth. If he hadn't been a man of the people, if he
hadn't had his living to earn, if he hadn't had more fun
in him than the writing of lyric poetry will satisfy! If it
was he made the English theatre, did not the theatre
make him what he is—what he might be to us?

Next come the clowns. It is necessary, I am ashamed
to say, to remark that Clown does not, first of all, mean
a person who tries to be funny. A clown is a countryman.
Now, your Cockney audience finds a countryman comic,
and your Cockney writer to this day often makes him
outrageously so. Shakespeare presumably knew something about countrymen, and he made the simple discovery and put it into practice for the first time in this
play that, set down lovingly, your clown is better fun by
far than mocked at; if indeed apart from an actor's
grimaces he had then been funny at all. Later on
Shakespeare did this, as he did most other things, better,
but he never did it so simply. If Shallow and Silence are
finer, they are different; moreover, though countrymen

they are not clowns. If Dogberry is as good, he hasn't, for me, quite the charm. There are little sketches in the last plays; that delightful person, for instance, at the end of *Antony and Cleopatra* with his, 'I wish you joy of the worm.' But from the moment Bottom, gloweringly mistrustful of poor Snug, asks, 'Let me play the lion, too', from that moment they have my heart, all five, for ever. It is a little puzzling to discover just how bad their play is meant to be. Did Quince write it? If he is guilty of 'Now am I dead', then, is not the prologue a plagiarism? But a good deal of more respectable playwriting than this was plagiarism, as who knew better than Shakespeare? I suspect he was of two minds himself on the point, if of any at all.

Then come the fairies. Can even genius succeed in putting fairies on the stage? The pious commentators say not. This play and the sublimer parts of *King Lear* are freely quoted as impossible in the theatre. But, then, by some trick of reasoning they blame the theatre for it. I cannot follow that. If a play written for the stage cannot be put on the stage the playwright, it seems to me, has failed, be he who he may. Has Shakespeare failed or need the producer only pray for a little genius, too? The fairies are the producer's test. Let me confess that, though mainly love of the play, yet partly, too, a hope of passing that test has inspired the present production. Foolhardy one feels facing it. But if a method of staging can compass the difficulties of *A Midsummer Night's Dream*, surely its cause is won.

Lacking genius one considers first how not to do a thing. Not to try and *realize* these small folk who war with rere-mice for their leathern wings, that goes without saying. In this play I can visualize neither a beginning nor an end to realism of either scenery or action. Nor yet to use children. To my mind neither children nor animals fit with the theatre. Perfect in their natural beauty, they put our artifice to shame. In this case one is tempted, one yields a little, over Cobweb and Co. It's possible, even probable, that children served Shakespeare. But I expect that the little eyasses of that time were as smartly trained in speaking verse as is a crack cathedral choir now in the singing of anthems. That there might be a special beauty, an impersonal clarity, in a boy's Oberon or Titania I can well believe. To take a nearly parallel case, who would not choose to hear treble rather than soprano through Bach's *Matthew Passion*? This is an interesting point, and it opens up the whole question of the loss and gain to pure poetry on the stage by the coming of women players. But where are our children with the training in fine speech and movement? Stop beneath the windows of an elementary school and listen. Or worse, listen to the chatter of a smart society gathering; in the school playground at least there is lung power. It will take some generations of awakening to the value of song and dance, tune and rhythm, to re-establish a standard of beauty in the English language.

The theatre might help if it were allowed. Though, first of all, heaven knows, it needs to help itself. One may say that the tradition of verse-speaking on the English stage is almost dead. So much the better. Our latest inheritance of it, at the least, was unsound, dating not from Shakespearean times, the great age of verse, but from the 'heroic' days of Rowe and Otway; later from the translators of 'the immortal Kotzebue'[2] and the portentous Sheridan Knowles.[3] Comic verse found its grave (at times a charmingly bedizened grave) in the rhymed burlesques of Planché[4] and Byron. But Shakespeare was a classic and must be spoken 'classically,' and what you couldn't speak classically you had better cut.

Look at the Shakespeare prompt books of even the last few years and see how mercilessly rhymed couplets were got rid of, blots upon the dignity of the play. From this sort of thing William Poel has been our saviour, and we owe him thanks. In the teeth of ridicule he insisted that for an actor to make himself like unto a human megaphone was to miss, for one thing, the whole merit of Elizabethan verse with its consonantal swiftness, its gradations sudden or slow into vowelled liquidity, its comic rushes and stops, with, above all, the peculiar beauty of its rhymes. We have had, of course, individual actors or speakers of taste and genius (one instances Forbes-Robertson), and there might be now and then a company inspired by such scholarly ideals as Benson could give, but Poel preached a gospel.

What else was Shakespeare's chief delight in this play but the screeds of word-music to be spoken by Oberon, Titania, and Puck? At every possible and impossible moment he is at it. For Puck's description of himself there may be need, but what excuse can we make for Titania's thirty-five lines about the dreadful weather except their sheer beauty? But what better excuse? Oberon is constantly guilty. So recklessly happy in writing such verse does Shakespeare grow that even the quarrel of the four lovers is stayed by a charming speech of Helena's thirty-seven lines long. It is true that at the end of it Hermia, her author allowing her to recollect the quarrel, says she is amazed at these passionate words, but that the passage beginning 'We, Hermia, like two artificial gods' is meant by Shakespeare to be spoken otherwise than with a meticulous regard to its every beauty is hard to believe. And its every beauty will scarcely shine through throbbing passion. No, his heart was in these passages of verse, and so the heart of the play is in them. And the secret of the play—the refutation of all doctrinaire criticism of it—lies in the fact that though they may offend against every letter of dramatic law they fulfil the inmost spirit of it, inasmuch as they are dramatic in themselves. They are instinct with that excitement, that spontaneity, that sense of emotional overflow which is drama. They are as carefully constructed for effective speaking as a messenger's speech in a Greek drama. One passage in particular, Puck's 'My mistress with a monster is in love', is both in idea and form, in its tension, climax, and rounding off, a true messenger's speech. Shakespeare, I say, was from the first a playwright in spite of himself. Even when he seems to sacrifice drama to poem he—instinctively or not—manages to make the poem itself more dramatic than the drama he sacrifices. And once he has found himself as a playwright very small mercy has he on verse for its own sake. He seems to write it as the fancy takes him, badly or well, broken or whole. Is there a single rule he will not break, lest his drama should for a moment suffer? Is there a supreme passage in the later plays but is supreme more in its dramatic emotion than its sheer poetry? Take for an extreme instance the line in *King Lear*, 'Never, never, never, never, never.' Can you defend it as poetry, any more than you can defend 'Oh, Sophonisba, Sophonisba, oh!'?[5] As a moment of drama what could be more poignantly beautiful? Whence comes the tradition that a blank verse play is, merely by virtue of its verse, the top notch of dramatic achievement? Shakespeare's best work, seen alive in the theatre, gives, I maintain, no colour to it. Verse was his first love, his natural medium—the finest medium for the theatre in general of his day, I'll admit. But how far he was, in principle and practice, from those worthy disciples who have for these centuries and do indeed still attempt to drag us wearily up their strictly decasyllabic pathway to

Parnassus, only a placing of their work and his side by side in the living theatre will show. It has all come, I suppose, from learned people elevating him to the study from the stage. Despite the theatre; it revenges itself. I digress.

The fairies cannot sound too beautiful. How should they look? One does one's best. But I realize that when there is perhaps no really right thing to do one is always tempted to do too much. One yields to the natural fun, of course, of making a thing look pretty in itself. They must be not too startling. But one wishes people weren't so easily startled. I won't have them dowdy. They mustn't warp your imagination—stepping too boldly between Shakespeare's spirit and yours. It is a difficult problem; we (Norman Wilkinson and I—he to do and I to carp) have done our best. One point is worth making. Oberon and Titania are romantic creations: sprung from Huron of Bordeaux, etc., say the commentators; come from the farthest steppe of India, says Shakespeare. But Puck is English folklore.

How should the fairies dance? Here I give up my part of apologist to Cecil Sharp. I only know they should have no truck with a strange technique brought from Italy in the eighteenth century. If there is an English way of dancing—and Sharp says there is—should not that be their way?

And what tunes should they sing to? English tunes. And on this point Sharp has much to say—more sometimes than I can quite follow him in.[6] I have no doubt there is a lyric missing at the end of the play, and to set a tune to the rhythm of Oberon's spoken words seems absurd. If this most appropriate one we borrow from *Two Noble Kinsmen* is not Shakespeare's (Swinburne thought it was), I'm sorry. I'm sorry, anyway, if it's vandalism, but something has to be done.

Finally, I divide the play into three parts. I don't defend the division; it only happens to be a convenient one. I can't defend any division, and some day I really must ask a modern audience to sit through two hours and a half of Shakespeare without a break; the play would gain greatly. This is less absurd, that is all, than the Jonsonian five act division of the Folio, for which, of course, there is no authority.

A Midsummer Night's Dream (1924)

PRE-EMINENTLY in three plays, in *A Midsummer Night's Dream, King Lear, Antony and Cleopatra*, Shakespeare's stagecraft is at issue with the mechanism of the modern theatre. It is an issue admitted, sometimes even perversely gloried in by editors; by the producer it is commonly evaded as far as may be. He has his modern audience to please and can plead this much excuse. But we in these prefaces must try at least to determine the issue and to analyze it, even though thereafter we can point to no solution but a compromise, and that an unsatisfactory one.

The issue for the three plays is not identical. In *King Lear* it is manifest in the greatness of the subject, in *Antony and Cleopatra* in the scope of the action. In *A Midsummer Night's Dream* it springs perhaps from the subject itself, more certainly from the necessities of its treatment as Shakespeare's stage determined them. Here is a play about fairies, about the adventures of four lovers and some rustics in a moonlit wood; and he wrote it for a theatre in which no visual illusion, as we interpret the term, was possible. His resource—all others beside it negligible—was the spoken word. No question of the wonders he works with this. Let us, however, with our modern theatre in mind, but before we yield to the charm of

> I know a bank where the wild thyme blows,
> Where oxlips and the nodding violet grows,

> Quite over-canopied with lush woodbine,
> With sweet musk-roses, and with eglantine:

and the rest—this magic stuff that Shakespeare pours not upon our eyes but in our ears—let us first note what he, very definitely, does *not* try to do.

We have grown accustomed to scenic productions of the play, and, of late years, almost as accustomed to protesting against them. And the dispute has apparently given birth to a perverse notion that we ought somehow to be able to make the best of both methods, that somewhere in Shakespeare's stagecraft the craft of the scenic stage is innate. This is surely a fallacy; does it need more than statement for its exposure?

> *Enter a fairy at one door and Robin Goodfellow at another,*

says the Folio. Shakespeare did not ask his audience to pretend to themselves that the doors were not there.

> Ill met by moonlight, proud Titania.

He did not expect them to shut their eyes upon the plain stage and visualize a moonlit glade.

He avoids the incongruous:

> I know a bank where the wild thyme blows.

It is not a bank which ought at that moment to be within sight and obviously isn't. No, our eyes may make sure of whatever is actually in front of them; Oberon in a fantastic dress, Puck bounding through a palpable doorway with his little western flower. For the rest—for how much, then!—the appeal is as directly to the ear as the appeal of a song or a symphony.

But to-day we are accustomed to the theatre of visual illusion. True, it is not deception we demand: at the age of ten or thereabout we cease to ask, 'Are they real trunks of trees?' The liking for make-believe lasts longer.

'So this is the forest of Arden.' Give us something that can be called ocular proof of it, if we are to give whole-hearted credit to Touchstone and Rosalind. But finally our need is aesthetic. The eye must be occupied and satisfied. It has been taught how to add its gains to the sum of the emotion a play can excite, and it has grown exigent. If it is not satisfied, it will turn traitor and frustrate the other senses.

But can we dress Shakespeare in a garment, however delightful, for which he made no allowance without cramping his play's action and obscuring its beauty? There has been much quarrelling round the question, between those who protest against any garment at all and those who are all for a garment, but at odds with each other—and most bitterly—as to the sort of garment it should be. The case against realistic scenery is a good one and never better than when this play is made the instance of it. Are we first to have Shakespeare's verse paint us the bank of wild thyme, nodding violet and musk-rose, and then let the scene-painter take his turn and show us a pretty picture so like the real thing that, 'By Jove,' we whisper (and while we whisper our distracted neighbours miss half a dozen lines of the play), 'you could almost pick those violets, couldn't you?' It will be admitted that to bring competing and discordant elements into the interpretation of any work of art is wrong. To avoid discordancy while satisfying still that hungry eye, modern producers have devised scenery which is not scenery, forests that are not like forests, and light that never was on sea or land. But have they thereby eliminated the competition too? That part of the question, in all its implications, is not so easy to answer, nor will the problem as a whole yield to logic. There are three parties to a dramatic performance, and each has its rights (and the scene-painter, if he is to be admitted, may make a fourth). The playwright devises, the actors interpret, and the rights of the audience are to a language of word and movement, which they can currently understand. Where all concerned are in familiar touch, no difficulty should arise. But in three hundred years even the theatre has seen changes. Shakespeare stands at one end of a road that has many turnings, and we at the other. He offers and asks for one thing; we are ready enough to offer and like another. How far will the new thing supplement the old, how far does it nullify it—that, roughly, is what one has to discover. In this play, for instance, he asks attention for his verse, for a little music, and allows for the eye only some simple costumed action and a little dancing upon a palpable stage. With these materials, within these bounds, his faculties at full stretch, he produces his play. Using these materials, kept within those bounds, and stretching our faculties of interpretation and appreciation to their full, we still—it is barely possible—may not be able to compass his vision and achieve his purposes, limited as they were. Change the materials, enlarge the bounds, and shall we not lose rather than gain? May not the beauty of a setting belittle the actor who is seen in it? Is the ear not cheated by delighting the eye? For the eye responds more easily, people look before they listen, we are naturally lazy, and our total faculty of attention is limited.

> Dark night that from the eye his function takes
> The ear more quick of apprehension makes.

The play itself has something to say upon the point.[7]

On the other hand here is our modern audience to be considered, with its justified demand for the use of conventions to which it is accustomed. The nearer we can all come, by use or study, to Shakespeare's own understanding of his art the better—that should be obvious. But the play, once it starts, must be so ordered as to yield us spontaneous enjoyment, even as it did—by conventions to which they were accustomed—to the audiences of three centuries ago.[8]

Here, then, is the issue and the producer's problem. This differs, of course, but in degree, not in kind, from that which every other play of Shakespeare must present to the modern stage. It is, by all appearances, the harder to solve, but, paradoxically, it may prove the more perfectly solvable. For, treat this play how you will, there is none whose interpretation must so much depend upon that unchartered individual quality we call taste. Perhaps Shakespeare's own production was a failure. He wrote no more of fairies, and he was not above trying to improve on a success. But it will be wise not to rely too much upon that possibility. And one piece of practical advice may be offered. Let the producer first bring his work to completion upon Shakespeare's own terms, and none other. If he can perfect the music of the poetry and the grace of the play's movement, not so much else will need doing. And in this preface we shall be concerned only with the play as Shakespeare's theatre might have staged it. The rest of the adventure, if it must be made, is a man's own affair. But when he had given the last inch of energy demanded, and devoted his imagination single-mindedly to Shakespeare's service, he should be aware enough of his author's purpose not, for the rest, to go so far wrong, one may suppose.

The Text and Act-Division

There are no important difficulties in the text; only a number of tiresome trifles have to be passed upon. Some few emendations force themselves upon us. But temptation merely to regularize the verse, where chance offers, had mostly better be resisted. The printer lapsed from full accuracy now and then, no doubt. But Shakespeare, even by this time, had come to prefer a dramatic effect, if only a tiny one, to a correctly rounded line.

The five act division is hardly a convenient one, if acts are to imply intervals and an audience going and coming. But there is this incidental interest in it. A stage-direction for the lovers, *They sleepe all the act*—that is, they remain asleep upon the stage during the interval between Acts III and IV—supplies us with one of the few pieces of evidence as to what an act-pause in the Elizabethan theatre might (but not by any means 'must') mean. If the actors lay there, it stands to reason that the interval, on this occasion, was not a very long one.

This carries us further. Act IV is short, but Act III is the longest of the five, and the two together make a large slice of the play. Therefore if they were played practically together, it is some sign, at least, that Elizabethan audiences were not hungry for intervals as we understand them. Perhaps they strolled in and out, intervals or no. The five act division had classic sanction. Whether the editors of the Folio imposed it on Shakespeare to lend him academic respectability, whether Shakespeare himself had, at times, or invariably, formally accepted it, scholars have not determined.[9] Our question, however, with the play's production involved, need only be: what dramatic validity have these divisions, do they rightly define the structure of the play?

A case can be made out for them. But then, with a method at once so flowing and so discursive as the Elizabethan stage allowed, half a dozen different plans for dividing up any play can be allowed dramatic purpose, and defended. Act I as it stands is a unit of action, plainly enough; so is Act V. But there is as good a dramatic case for a pause after Act III, Scene i, as at the end of Act II. Again, a pause after Act III may be effective; but, as we have seen, it is, on an Elizabethan stage, technically inconvenient. And if, with the resources of the modern stage to rely upon, this consideration is to be ruled out, then a pause—on the whole as effective in itself, and dramatically far more purposeful—could be made after Oberon, Titania and Puck depart in the middle of Act IV, Scene i. Modern producers, as it happens, see at this point—and generally take—an opportunity for a prolonged sunrise to slow music while the lovers and Bottom lie sleeping. For the music they may plead Shakespeare; though if, as is possible, the lovers had slept 'all the act' to a musical accompaniment but a few minutes earlier, he is unlikely to have repeated the effect. But an interval, falling here, would leave a most inadequate fourth act, which is short even as it now stands.

And so one can argue, in this play as in others, for and against this division and that. The general conclusion will be, one may suggest, that on the Elizabethan stage the act-division was a matter of practical convenience. Shakespeare constructed a play according to a certain plan, or at least developed it to some rhythm. He may sometimes—perhaps in *King Lear*, in *Antony and Cleopatra*—have had the classic five-act form in mind; oftener there is intrinsic evidence that he had not. It is possible that in the theatres four formal pauses were made. When intervals as we understand them were in question, it is as possible that these were let depend upon convenience for the shifting of properties, the changing of costumes, the doubling of parts, and the like. Moreover there is evidence that, if a play were shifted from one type of stage to another, intervals (and even formal pauses, therefore) might, for convenience' sake, be redistributed, rhythm of construction and dramatic effect being counted as of not much importance or held to be not much affected in the process.

This, if it be allowed, should at least free the modern producer from any sort of slavery to the five acts of the Folio. He must then abide by whatever rhythm of construction he divines in the play; and 'the fewer intervals the better' is a good general rule with a play that needs to transport its audiences into a mood of fancy and to hold them there, yet does not strain their emotions. Much is to be said with this play for treating Act I as a prelude, then for giving Acts II, III, IV with no break. Act V has every claim to stand separate, though the second scene of Act IV can, if convenient, be quite legitimately tacked to it.

Nor need the producer concern himself, in this connection, with the play's 'time analysis,' upon which thought and ink have been wasted in plenty. The duration of the action is planned for four days. This is stated to begin with, and so emphatically stated that we are obviously meant to remark it. And the dramatic worth of the matter lies, of course, in the need for giving Hermia some clearly stated and limited time in which to make choice of her fate. Shakespeare knows the value of a firm jumping-off place. Thereafter the matter loses its importance for him, and he becomes—we may disrespectfully surmise—correspondingly careless about its regulation. The adventures in the wood are *in effect* the adventures of one night. When Theseus wakes the lovers, he states that the four days are up—and who is there that would contradict such a benevolent hero? Nor does it matter to Hermia, for her troubles are over. Nor does the audience notice a discrepancy, nor did Shakespeare care, nor need the play's producer.

The Staging

We can extract from the text and the directions one or
two bits of evidence as to the play's staging in Shakespeare's time; they may help to show the modern producer when it will and will not prove yielding to the
importunity of his own circumstances.

There is a story that the play was written to be
performed at some great marriage festivity. What a
wedding present! And—though the text as we have it
may show addition—the story is a likely one. There is
the fitness of the fable, the play's whole tone and atmosphere, the appropriate ending. Further, there are small
signs of some later adaptation to the public stage.[10]
Between Acts III and IV comes that stage-direction for
the lovers, *They sleepe all the act.* No such direction is given
for Titania between Acts II and III. Why? Possibly—
probably!—because her bower was the inner stage and
could be concealed throughout an interval with curtains.[11]
But that sleeping *all the act* is a clumsy business, whose-
ever the responsibility for it. The lovers must lie on the
outer, the open stage. They cannot be crowded together;
besides, the inner stage will be needed a dozen lines
later. But it does not look as if any dramatist would in
his play's first planning have let himself and his actors
in for such an awkward few minutes.

Right upon this comes:

> *Enter Queen of Fairies, and Clowne, and Fairies, and the
> King behind them*

According to the Quartos Oberon remains behind them
till Bottom is asleep, when Puck enters to him; according
to the Folio he must go off at some unstated moment,
for we have

> *Enter Robin Goodfellow and Oberon.*

What is the point of the change? Probably that, the exposition of sleep having come upon him, Bottom must be retired to the inner stage, or he will be sadly in the way when Theseus and Hippolyta appear and wake the lovers. Oberon, therefore, cannot stay *behind them*. But when the Quarto copy was made he could.

There is like evidence in Act III, Scene i, of some change in the circumstances of staging, and again Titania's bower is concerned. Part of the confusion may be due to the printer's errors. But it does look as if the apparition of Bottom with the ass-head did not at first involve his entrance; and is there—or not—a peculiar insistence upon 'this hawthorn brake'?

These are flimsy matters upon which to found any theory. But now consider the play's construction as a whole. No use is made, except thus confusedly, of the ordinary stage resources of a public theatre. Picture, on the other hand, the great hall of an Elizabethan mansion, with the two doors in the screen at its end. These provide exit and entrance enough.[12] Imagine such a 'machine' as was commonly used for masques, carried in or pushed forward for the fairy scenes to serve as a hawthorn brake and Titania's bower, carried out or pushed back when they were over; imagine some 'banks' disposed around for the lovers to sleep on, and chairs and benches brought in for the audience of the 'most lamentable comedy'. Into such a setting it will be found that the general action of the play and even its detailed business most conveniently fit.

Not that we are called upon to-day to reproduce these exact circumstances even if they were those of its original production. But they may suggest to us the particular kinds of effect that Shakespeare looked for in the play's interpretation.

The 'machine' gave no illusion, that goes without saying. It was a pretty, perhaps fantastic piece of decoration, which enabled Titania to lie hid while other scenes passed, from which, possibly, Bottom protruded his ass-head to the terror of his fellows, who were so innocently regarding their tiring house, expecting his re-entry from it. And its exchange for the inner stage or for whatever substitute a modern theatre may provide need make little more than mechanical difference. But what will count for far more will be the intimacy of the whole affair and the qualities of performance which intimacy allows and makes effective. And this is worth more than passing consideration. There is no play of Shakespeare's that demands (the clowns' scenes apart, and even these should be simply done) such sustained delicacy of treatment. Story and characters both are kept—are constantly being reined—within the bounds of gentleness. The verse has the virtues of chamber music. It is never robustly declamatory; it asks constantly for a quiet clarity of utterance; it offers chance after chance for the most delicate phrasing. And nothing can compensate for the lack or the loss of all this. There are no opportunities for vigorous acting as the Elizabethans understood it, and violence, assertiveness, any mere noise will break the whole fabric. Egeus is allowed to create no more than will provide a lively contrast to Duke Theseus' magnanimity (and serve as a warning to stern parents in the audience not to make themselves ridiculous when love-affairs are in hand). Puck's boisterousness is but that of a naughty child. The four-handed lovers' quarrel is turned to amusing futility. But we have:

> . . . O happy fair,
> Your eyes are lode-stars and your tongue's sweet air,
> More tuneable than lark to shepherd's ear,
> When wheat is green, when hawthorn buds appear.

Fair love, you faint with wandering in the wood;
And to speak troth, I have forgot our way;
We'll rest us, Hermia, if you think it good,
And tarry for the comfort of the day.

Be kind and courteous to this gentleman;
Hop in his walks, and gambol in his eyes;
Feed him with apricocks, and dewberries,
With purple grapes, green figs, and mulberries;
The honey-bags steal from the humble-bees,
And, for night-tapers, crop their waxen thighs,
And light them at the fiery glow-worm's eyes,
To have my love to bed, and to arise;
And pluck the wings from painted butterflies,
To fan the moon-beams from his sleeping eyes:
Nod to him, elves, and do him courtesies.

         . . . damned spirits all,
That in cross-ways and floods have burial,
Already to their wormy beds are gone;
For fear lest day should look their shames upon,
They wilfully themselves exile from light,
And must for aye consort with black-brow'd night.
But we are spirits of another sort;
I with the morning's love have oft made sport;
And, like a forester, the groves may tread,
Even till the eastern gate, all fiery-red,
Opening on Neptune with fair blessed beams,
Turns into yellow gold his salt green streams.

My hounds are bred out of the Spartan kind,
So flew'd, so sanded; and their heads are hung
With ears that sweep away the morning dew;
Crook-knee'd, and dew-lapp'd like Thessalian bulls;
Slow in pursuit, but match'd in mouth like bells,
Each under each.

Wherever and however the play was first performed, whether by candlelight to a kindly company—to just such a company as Duke Theseus himself would have gathered into just such a hall—or whether it did first face the daylight and distraction of a public theatre, such verse must gain by gracious treatment and response, even as the music of stringed instruments is mellowed in an old panelled room.

The Music and Dancing

For long, Mendelssohn's music to the play, charming in itself, seemed to have acquired a prescriptive right to be used. But, apart from the question of intrinsic suitability, it involves a quite unallowable treatment of the text; involves, besides, the practical suppression of the lyrics. 'You spotted snakes', for instance, might be written in German or Choctaw for any sense that the cleverest singer of it to this music can make for the keenest listener.

The whole problem, Mendelssohn dismissed, has been argued acutely and with authority by Mr Cecil Sharp, who, moreover, was able to put his conclusions very successfully to the test. He decided for folk-song and dance, though it must be owned that his arguments might well have led another man elsewhere. Country dance, however, if not folk-dance, is thrust on us by the text, by Titania's

> If you will patiently dance in our round...
> Come now a roundel, and a fairy song.

Nor is the ditty which is to be sung and danced by the light of the dead and drowsy fire likely to differ greatly from this. And a bergomask is a bergomask.

But as to the music itself, Mr Sharp broaches the question of music for Shakespeare's plays in general,[13] and it is over this that though diffidently, I must join issue with him. He suggests three possible methods of providing it; of these rejects, first, the adaptation of Elizabethan music originally set to other words, second, the composing of music in the Elizabethan idiom, and prefers original composition. He does so on the broad ground that though 'Shakespeare the man was an Elizabethan; Shakespeare the artist and the dramatist belongs to all time', and says that 'To us Elizabethan music always sounds strange, unfamiliar, archaic—and, to some extent, precious.'

It seems such wholesome doctrine that one is loth to reject it. But, in practice, will not the modern musician, thus encouraged to 'be himself', be to Shakespeare very much what most other modern collaborators have been, working by such encouragement;—painters, limelighters, costumiers, crying out, 'Not for an age, but for all time', and smothering him with their enthusiastic contributions to his glory? Now and then one might find a composer, the quality of whose art, its values of emotion and form, had about that relation to Shakespeare's own for which he allowed in the nicely calculated opportunities he gave for collaboration between the two. Shakespeare knew something about music, it appears; he had, at least, rather more than a 'reasonable good ear for the tongs and bones.' We must suppose therefore that he imagined, pretty justly, the precise quality that was to be produced when Oberon began,

> Come, my Queen, take hands with me,
> And rock the ground whereon these sleepers be,

and to be produced almost as much by the accompanying music as the words themselves.

Music, even as Drama, has developed new resources and found new methods in three hundred years. One does Shakespeare ill service by setting his plays in visual surroundings which, being designed for other modes of dramatic expression, necessarily deform them. Is it much better to blanket them with sounds as foreign?

If, as Mr Sharp says, Elizabethan music *does* sound archaic and too unfamiliar to the modern ear, then, by the sound plea that a play must provide spontaneous enjoyment, there is a case for compromise between past and present—though this may but lead us to his rejected (wisely rejected, as I think) composing of music in Elizabethan idiom. But the letting loose of modern musicians with a recommendation to do their damn'dest will, for the moment, almost certainly result in tyrannous noise. I should myself have thought (though necessarily in such a matter I speak under correction) that here, precisely, was an opportunity for leading an audience back, and all unconsciously, into that medium of sound, of emotion even, in which the play was first meant to make its effect. It is just because Elizabethan music *is* somewhat unfamiliar to the ear that I advocate it. It will not surely strike the uninstructed hearer so strangely as to provoke argument or raise questions; and the instructed hearer can probably take the appropriate sort of pleasure in it. Music affects most of us without our well knowing why. Moreover there is no art that can so readily, by suggestion, and even by its very unfamiliarity, transport us over time and space, though the destination be barely known. Bagpipes suggest Scotland, a guitar Italy, a tomtom the jungle. A minuet will set us imagining eighteenth-century surroundings. We may lack the knowledge to place Byrd and Dowland in theirs, but the surroundings in this case are supplied by the play. We have only to surrender to the sounds.

Music, truly, is of its time; and there is innate in it something of the spirit and behaviour of its time, which could never perhaps find equal expression in words. Words are for thoughts, and emotion must be framed in terms of thought before words will convey it. But music may express something, now as simple as set movements of the body, now as subtle as those moods of the mind and the measures to which emotion learns to beat. By reasoning about it we may make it more strange than it ever need be if we simply listen. For the emotional self is apter at shifting ground than the intellectual, apter to explode unknown ground.[14] I am sure at least that you can sing and dance a man back into the seventeenth century far more easily than you can argue him there. And I cannot think that any approach to listening with Shakespeare's ears is other than a gain. One of the ways to a love of his verse may well be through the music that he loved.

For *A Midsummer Night's Dream* itself, however, Mr Sharp finds a fourth plan which does not conflict with my theories and (he will forgive me) saves him the application of his own. He chooses folk-music—'which is impervious to the passage of time and will satisfy equally the artistic ideals of every age ... It is undated, it belongs to no period; it is a growth, not a composition.' From pure liking I agree that for the fairy roundels, Bottom's courageous carolling, and for the Bergomask nothing better can be found than folk-music. It has its roots in the ages; it must have sounded familiarly in Shakespeare's ears, as it still, at first hearing, sounds somehow familiar to us. One might pedantically call its use for Oberon's 'still music' into question, but unity of effect will excuse this. For other plays, though, folk-music will not serve; and then Mr Sharp and I must find ourselves at honest odds.

Two particular points need remark. The fairy song for the last scene is missing; of that there is little doubt, and somehow one must be supplied. The expedient (Mendelssohn's) of setting Oberon's and Titania's two speeches to music instead is a poor one, and Capell is surely right when he condemns the Folio's printing of Oberon's speech, 'Now until the break of day', following the song as the song itself. The producer, therefore, in his difficulty will search Shakespeare for another appropriate lyric. If he cannot find one (and I think he cannot), he must turn, as it may be Shakespeare did, elsewhere. It so happens, however, that a play with which Shakespeare's own name has been traditionally associated, *The Two Noble Kinsmen*, has in it a wedding song not unlike his own work, nor quite unworthy of him.

> Roses, their sharp spines being gone,
> Not royal in their smell alone
>   But in their hue;
> Maiden pinks, of odour faint,
> Daisies smell-less, yet most quaint,
>   And sweet thyme true;
>
> Primrose, firstborn child of Ver,
> Merry spring-time's harbinger
>   With her bells dim;
> Ox-lips in their cradles growing,
> Marigolds on deathbeds blowing,
>   Larks'-heels trim.
>
> All dear Nature's children sweet,
> Lie 'fore bride and bridegroom's feet,
>   Blessing their sense!
> Not an angel of the air,
> Bird melodious or bird fair,
>   Be absent hence!

The crow, the slenderous cuckoo, nor
The boding raven, nor chough hoar,
        Nor chattering pie,
May on our bride-house perch or sing,
Or with them any discord bring,
        But from it fly!

In default of better this may serve.[15]

The *Musicke Tongs, Rurall Musicke* of the Folio (Act IV, Scene i) may fairly be held suspect. Not to speak of its absence from the Quartos, the run of the text here almost forbids any such interruption. The only likely occasion for it is when Peas-blossom and company have been dismissed. There would be a pleasing, fantastic irony in little Titania and her monster being lulled to sleep by the distant sound of the tongs and the bones; it would make a properly dramatic contrast to the 'still music' for which she calls a moment later, her hand in Oberon's again. A producer might, without offence, venture on the effect. (But Oberon, by the way, had better stop the noise with a disgusted gesture before he begins to speak.)

And the winding of the horns that follows should be quite elaborately symphonic. This is Shakespeare's picturing of sunrise.

The Costume

A designer finds himself with a fairly free hand; and the freer he keeps it, within the bounds of discretion, the better. He should not, that is to say, let himself be entrapped by the word 'Athens' into any chilly and so-called classical precision. Duke Theseus has no closer relation to his historical namesake than has Oberon to Louis Quatorze. The sounding names Hippolyta Perigenia,

Ariadne, the talk of Diana's altar and of hounds of Sparta, and of coming a conqueror from Thebes, were still romantic in Elizabethan ears and called up figures moving in some 'once upon a time'. Does our imagination respond differently to-day? Can we not hear

> Call Philostrate.
> Here, mighty Theseus.
> Say what abridgement have you for this evening?
> What masque? what music? . . .

without the classic names obliterating the Elizabethan phrase? Well, let the figures of the two, as we are to see them staged, allow as much for our susceptibilities as will not mean the re-drawing or discolouring of the imaginative picture of the play as it was first made. Here is the designer's problem, so far as one exists. He will further have to contrive some unity of effect. For Oberon and Titania are, it appears, as at home in India as in Athens. Puck begins to smack of Warwickshire. And though Quince and his fellows may work for bread upon Athenian stalls, as we hear them talk it does not seem as if they would be strangers, quite, in Stratford market-place.

The Casting and Acting

The cast falls roughly into three groups: that of Theseus and the lovers, the fairies, the clowns. To the first two falls the speaking of the verse; for this purpose they must be thought of together.

While it would be misleading to speak of a musical range of voices wanted, from *basso* for Theseus to *soprano* for Titania,—for that would be to formalize the matter unduly to the prejudice of individual character—nevertheless one should have in mind some such structure of tone. In any play it will count as a means of marking its form, of giving contrast between part and part, and of making scene succeeding scene the fresher to the ear. And in this play it will count more than in most.

Hints—fortuitously dropped, no doubt—of the importance Shakespeare might attach to a characteristic quality of voice and to beauty of speech generally are not lacking in the plays. Lear's tribute to Cordelia is in everyone's mind. Part of Helena's prettily envious praise of her rival is of a

> tongue's sweet air,
> More tuneable than lark to shepherd's ear.

And the very tone in which Hippolyta must tell us that once in a wood of Crete she bay'd the boar with hounds of Sparta till

> ... every region near
> Seem'd all one mutual cry: I never heard
> So musical a discord, such sweet thunder;

and Theseus' answer that his hounds are

> ... match'd in mouth like bells,
> Each under each,

—the very words seem to suggest such matching of their own tones.[16] But no hints should be needed to tell us how vital is this question of right relation between the voices. One must beware of pushing the comparison with music too far; but to neglect this would be as if one should leave the parts in a symphony to the lot of any instruments that might come handy.

Take the very first scene. It opens with the formal serenity of Theseus' and Hippolyta's speeches; mellow-toned—note the sounds of the vowels in

> Now, fair Hippolyta, our nuptial hour
> Draws on apace.

Impinging on this comes the shrill rattle of Egeus with his

> ... rings, gawds, conceits,
> Knacks, trifles, nosegays, sweet-meats; ...

Next, Hermia's meek obstinacy, rhythmical, distinct, low:

> I do entreat your grace to pardon me.
> I know not by what power I am made bold;
> Nor how it may concern my modesty,
> In such a presence here to plead my thoughts.

Then Demetrius and Lysander strike each his note. Demetrius, slow, hard-bitten, positive, pleasantly surly— not much romance in this young man.

> Relent, sweet Hermia;—and, Lysander, yield
> Thy crazed title to my certain right.

And Lysander, glib and impertinent, melodious, light:

> You have her father's love, Demetrius;
> Let me have Hermia's: do you marry him.

Fine spirit in him too, though; for he says his say to the Duke, bates not a point of it, rings it out confident and clear. The measured speech and mellow voice of Theseus now modulate the scene back to the tone it began upon. Then he departs with his train and the lovers are left alone.

The passage which follows must be one of the most charming things that Shakespeare ever wrote. It is besides (such appraisement being somewhat profitless) typical of the play in quality and method both; better than charming, it is typically right.

LYSANDER. How now, my love? Why is your cheek so pale?
  How chance the roses there do fade so fast?
HERMIA.   Belike for want of rain; which I could well
  Beteem them from the tempest of mine eyes.
LYSANDER. Ah me! for aught that ever I could read,
  Could ever hear by tale or history,
  The course of true love never did run smooth!
  But, either it was different in blood;
HERMIA.   O cross! too high to be enthrall'd to low!
LYSANDER. Or else misgraffed, in respect of years;
HERMIA.   O spite! too old to be engag'd to young!
LYSANDER. Or else it stood upon the choice of friends:
HERMIA.   O hell! to choose love by another's eye!
LYSANDER. Or, if there were a sympathy in choice,
  War, death, or sickness did lay siege to it;
  Making it momentary as a sound,
  Swift as a shadow, short as any dream;
  Brief as the lightning in the collied night,
  That, in a spleen, unfolds both heaven and earth,
  And ere a man hath power to say,—Behold!
  The jaws of darkness do devour it up:
  So quick bright things come to confusion.

The whole passage is conventional in form. Conceit
answers conceit. The pretty antiphony is convention
itself. Lysander's apologue is conventionally rounded and
complete. But how nicely it is charged with emotion,
with enough to illumine the form, but not with so much,
nor of such a complexity as would warp it. Hence it is
dramatically right; that is to say, the matter and manner
are at one.

Note the intimate tenderness to which Lysander's first
bravado has turned. The two are alone in a yet unfriend-
ly world. Not a tragic world though, for Theseus had
straightway suggested the softening of the rebellious

young lady's punishment—at the worst to a vowing of austerity and single life. They can be playfully wistful about their hard fate. And as the scene ripples on, Hermia springs to cheerfulness as delicately as she had fallen to grief; the way out is so easy; in a minute she is bantering her lover.

Now comes Helena, wistful and troubled in her turn, her first speech matching Lysander's plaint of the course of true love. Another antiphony to follow, lightly comic this time, Hermia chirping her disdainful triumph, Helena drooping to defeated silence. Then, one at each side, the two lovers start to cheer Helena with the tale of their own good luck to be, their thoughts and voices alike in tune. Oblivious of her silence they go their ways; and she is left to protest, prettily, fancifully and spiritedly— there being no target near now for her humility—of her fate, and to flash on a plan not of happiness, but of the next best thing, of an even better thing for the purposes of comedy, redoubled woe. So the scene ends.

It is ill anatomizing such delicate stuff—the dissection of a butterfly! But this is how butterfly flights must be achieved in the theatre, where nothing is natural that is not made first by study, then by forgetfulness, to appear so.

Well, what does the dissection first serve to show? To say that the sense of the scene springs from its sound would, of course, be absurd. But it is remarkable how much sheer sound, in quality, contrast, change, is made to contribute. Make as much of the stark meaning of it all as you will; if the scene is sung to the wrong tunes (the comparison is, for once, irresistible), if the time is not adjusted, if the discords and harmonies are not valued, its essential character will be obscured and lost. This must be to some extent true of any play; in the interpretation of *A Midsummer Night's Dream* it is the dominating truth. For Shakespeare has sacrificed every other more purely dramatic advantage to this one. He allows himself no absorbing complexity of plot, no development of character. Nothing—it was his mood—may mar or cloud the limpid music of his verse. Development of character, indeed, his scheme in any case forbids. There can be little of it under enchantment. Human promptings do certainly bring the lovers to the wood, but once there they are spell-bound. No one but Oberon remains master of himself, and fairy psychology would seem to be of the simplest.[17] But is it not all meant to appear only as the fierce vexation of a dream? Even so—even within these limits—Shakespeare forswears the strong contrasts of personality which are the stepping stones of a play's progress and can make the conflict of its scenes more forcible. He has occasion, that is to say, for the merely fantastic incongruity of Bottom wound in Titania's arms. But, having once outlined his Hermia and Helena, Demetrius and Lysander, he makes little enough play with their likeness or unlikeness till he needs some material for fun in a squabble.

Nor does the verse itself, as a rule, hold any extreme effects of light and shade. It has neither sharp turns of phrase, nor sudden checking of pace, nor one twisted or tortured thought. It flows on like a river in sunlight. When a particular effect is wanted we are more likely to find it made by purely poetic means. We have the change to a tenser metre for Puck and Oberon when the magic of the love-juice is in question, or when Puck is dancing with suppressed excitement. We have the pretty use of a quatrain to emphasize the drowsy happiness in which Hermia and Lysander wander through the wood; the use of quatrain and couplet and a four times repeated rhyme when there is need to stress the increasing delusion of the lovers—this sudden pleasant artificiality does somehow help to.

In fine, Shakespeare has a theme, which only poetry can fully illuminate, and he trusts to poetry. Nor will he risk any conflict of interest, all the rest of his dramatist's equipment must cry small for the occasion. Wherefore we in our turn must plan the play's interpretation upon these terms. Poetry, poetry; everything to serve and nothing to compete with it!

Should Oberon and Titania differ from the mortals by any trick of speech?[18] Shakespeare has made little provision for it. He allots, as we have seen, a small amount of short metre verse to them and to Puck. There is in thus much strangeness a certain suggestion of their fairy status, and it is to be noted that after their reconciliation to the sound of the 'still music' comes

> PUCK. Fairy king, attend, and mark;
>   I do hear the morning lark.
> OBERON. Then, my queen, in silence sad,
>   Trip we after the night's shade:
>   We the globe can compass soon,
>   Swifter than the wand'ring moon.
> TITANIA. Come, my lord; and in our flight,
>   Tell me how it came this night,
>   That I sleeping here was found
>   With these mortals, on the ground.

The lilt, no less than the meaning, helps to express them to us as beings other than mortal, treading the air. And still more significant, of course, is the use of the same metre when they come with their train to bless the bride-beds. Its lightness, its strange simplicity, give them to just as much supernatural dignity as is right and no more. For they are fairies, not gods. But all this the metre itself will all but accomplish, let the actor only yield himself to it. He certainly must not by anything he may do violate the general harmony of the verse.

Oberon's squabble with Titania stands, of course, as counterpart to the lovers' quarrelling. The fairy couple are indeed (and if the play was written for the occasion of a wedding the point is more pertinent) gibbeted as a comically awful warning of what marriage may turn to if jealousy and temper get the upper hand. But, paying due respect to their majesties, and the better to accommodate such distasteful matters in a story that is to end in a triple bridal, they are made merely daintily ridiculous. Titania and Theseus! Oberon and Hippolyta! What childish nonsense! And to make each other miserable, all for the sake of a little Indian boy! Sensible human beings never behave like that—unless they are bewitched.

There may be, then, even such a slight air of travesty about the two, even as the four lovers, being bewitched, will lightly travesty their saner selves. But is Oberon's fairy disposition so strange to us after all? Certainly he is very outspoken. Without a blush he says,

> Thou shalt not from this grove
> Till I torment thee for this injury.

A moment later, how the callousness of Demetrius shocks him! No matter, a little magic will put all right. And then, as this goes wrong, a little more magic. For he does not take very long views or pause to consider what may be round the corner, and what he wants he must have done instanter and without question. He has next to see the terrible results of his good intentions, watches in stupefied silence the four poor mortals brought even to tears and to blows. Then he bethinks himself and turns again to his Titania. Even so, he'll not forgive her unless he gets his way. He must taunt her at his pleasure, and she in mild terms beg his patience. But every now and then passion and self-will are lost in a serene self-forgetfulness. For a moment amidst the jarring the

beauty of a flower or the thought of the shining moon
will absorb him. And always behind his busy inconse-
quence there dwells the sense—

> But we are spirits of another sort:
> I with the morning's love have oft made sport...

All very fairy-like and outlandish! Yet the ironic ear may
catch a more familiar echo.

There is hint, though, of a magic wiser than Oberon's,
and potent to do us mortals a good turn after all. For
hear Demetrius:

> ...I wot not by what power
> (But by some power it is) my love to Hermia,
> Melted as is the snow, seems to me now
> As the remembrance of an idle gaud,
> Which in my childhood I did dote upon;
> And all the faith, the virtue of my heart,
> The object, and the pleasure of mine eye,
> Is only Helena.

He wots not by what power, no more do we, no more
does Shakespeare. Had he chosen, instead of playing
fairy pranks, to write a whole serious play round the
question he might still have left it unanswered.

There may be then, we said, a touch of travesty about
Oberon. But the word still implies something too clumsy
for his fairyhood. It is rather that he is in everything, as
one says, just a little too good to be true. He is kinglier
than Theseus, more gallant far than Lysander, more
despicably jealous than Demetrius, but with a con-
scienceless ease that makes it all a little unreal. We
should smile at him as we are apt to smile at long past
romantic visions of ourselves.

So—yet not quite so—with Titania. She is Nature's
spoiled darling when things go well; when things go ill

with her, all Nature falls into discord. But how she has her way! Flowers and beasts and birds must serve her; and let none of her fairy court be absent for more than a third part of a minute on her errands, or she'll know the reason why. She can do no wrong. What more monstrous than her infatuation for Bottom of the ass's head! What more indelicate than her approaches to him! But Peas-blossom, Cobweb, Moth, Mustardseed and the rest accept the situation without demur. And so must we. Whatever Titania does, she must do so beautifully that it will seem right. While she lavishes her favours on the clumsy fellow, she must almost make us see him with her own enchanted eyes. Not indeed till her silver tongue is silenced and the two fall asleep can we, with the repentant Oberon, realize the horrid truth. Yes, if Titania is ridiculous, we worship her the more for that. See what it means to be a fairy queen.

Upon the reconciliation, though, the touch of travesty must vanish.

> Sound music. Come, my queen, take hands with me,
> And rock the ground whereon these sleepers be.
> Now thou and I are new in amity;
> And will, to-morrow midnight, solemnly,
> Dance in duke Theseus' house triumphantly,
> And bless it to all fair posterity.

And when they come in their dainty majesty, as unheralded as happiness, they must seem to us as simply and naturally beautiful.

The fairy court is certainly no place for idlers. In Titania's service, who could find time to come down off his tiptoes! Peas-blossom and the rest are ever a-hover waiting for commands to blow them hither and thither. Their business is revelry and every other sort of delightful uselessness; and desperately busy they are kept about it

Over hill, over dale,
Through bush, through briar,
Over park, over pale,
Through flood, through fire,
I do wander everywhere,
Swifter than the moon's sphere . . .
I must go seek some dew-drops here,
And hang a pearl in every cowslip's ear.

The cue is given us immediately. How, with our human material, to gain the effect is another matter. Not—we will always hope—by ingenious machinery, gauzes, lighting. Such toys are attractive enough in themselves. Shakespeare, it would seem, fell a victim on occasion to such as he could command; whether a willing or unwilling one, who shall say? But he never turned them to any very remarkable dramatic account; and in this play, quite clearly, he made no allowance for them at all. They are apt to become, then, but an excuse for neglecting the means that are provided.

We do seem to need children, and it is to be supposed that Shakespeare made use of them. Oberon may overtop his subjects, as the king's figure in an ancient painting is drawn to a measure beyond that of ordinary mortals. But bulky fairies simply will not do. What Shakespeare probably did have at his command was a troop of youths excellently trained to speak and sing and move and dance.[19] It is training that is needed; no mere drill through a set of rehearsals, but such training as a dancer gives to his feet and a pianist to his fingers. A producer may manoeuvre his fairies according to judgment and taste, but, to begin with, the exact beauty of their demeanour must be a fitting counterpart to all the beauty of speech the play asks for. The one is, in fact, the proper complement to the other.[20]

Puck accounts himself a fairy, and on the whole we must take his word for it. But he emphasizes the fact so boastfully as to suggest that he is at least of another and inferior breed. He is always boasting and swaggering and confidently doing the wrong thing. He bubbles over with incongruous self-importance. He can't go off to pick a flower without remarking that he could—if Oberon should happen to prefer it—girdle the earth for him in forty minutes. Nevertheless, one suspects him to be quite unacquainted with 'the farthest steppe of India'. His range is the Athenian woods (or, it may better be, the county of Warwick). He is a rustic sprite, and his notions of a joke betray it. When Oberon comes 'into residence' he has a tremendous time, showing off his latest tricks, basking—or rather leaping and bounding—in the sun of royal patronage. But, Oberon departed, poor Puck is probably reduced to playing tricks on dairy-maids, has no one but himself to boast to, waits wistfully for the next golden hour to strike. He is of no age, but if he were human he would be young. What his speech may lack in fine tone it makes up for in rhythm. His rougher, rustic touch is in valuable contrast with Oberon and the lovers. He spins the play on its course.

As parts for acting the four lovers have never been highly regarded. As characters they necessarily suffer, we saw, by being sport for Oberon's magic most of the time. But the more the play's interpreting is let depend on the charm of its verse, the better the place, naturally, that the four will find in it, for, between them, they run the compass of its beauty. This apart though, there is some excellent fun in the writing of them; and each has personality enough, and there is contrast enough between all four, to make the weaving in and out of their adventures effective. And the meting of some measure of poetic justice in this process makes their case the more interesting. Hermia, as vain of her rejected lover—for all she's so off-hand about him!—as she is confident of Lysander, has a rude shock when they both turn from her. Nor does she take this over prettily, as Helena, it must be owned, is a little over-ready to point out to her. And Helena, too, is paid out in her own coin. Mock-modesty is her pose. Then when Lysander and Demetrius compete in adoration for her, she can only believe that they are mocking her too. But Helena is so well-aware of herself that one might almost suspect her of a sense of humour. She sets Demetrius in pursuit of Hermia only to 'enrich her pain'; pursuing him herself, it is hard to believe that she does not enjoy the extreme embarrassment her attentions cause him. This really is a most subtle revenge on Demetrius. And when it comes to argument,—poor thick-headed fellow, he's helpless. At last he reproaches her with immodesty; and that seems a sound stroke. But she retorts that his well-known virtue allows any woman to feel safe with him, a compliment—and surely she need not have put it that way—to which under the circumstances there is no effective reply. And what can make a man more ridiculous than to find himself running away from a woman through a wood in the dark, and to find, moreover, that she can run as fast as he?

This scene, and others, abound in the humour of raillery. They owe their distinction to the musical charm of the verse and the fancy of the images; they are a little too dependent therefore upon nicety of speaking to gain their full effect in any theatre where this is not given pride of place. But, as we have seen, this is true of three quarters of the play. It is true certainly of the pretty duet, with its rhymes and its riddling, between Hermia and Lysander before they lie down to sleep. And Lysander's cool repudiation of her, when the love-juice has worked upon him, must lose half its point unless the slight caricature of the easy charming melodic swing of his former love-making is recognizable; and this implies a delicacy of treatment for both, not easily come by, nor, it must be confessed, likely to appeal to any but sensitive ears. Trained actors ask a trained audience; however, the one earns the other. Clumsier Demetrius, at the first moment of his enchanted waking, caricatures himself, too; out-caricatures Lysander; he pirouettes in jack-boots. No wonder poor Helena cries out:

> . . . I see you all are bent
> To set against me for your merriment.

This scene, thus absurdly begun, gathering complexity with Hermia's arrival, brings the mischief to its full pitch. Oberon, the somewhat astonished author of it, is, we must remember, spectator of the whole, the silently chuckling Robin Goodfellow at his feet. Within the limitation of its method the scene is amazingly well furnished in diversified effect. Long passages of poetry for Helena sustain the play's beauty and romance—as well as our sentimental interest in the unenchanted fortunes of the four—and they are abruptly followed and set off by the young men's fatuous wrangling. Demetrius, easily outclassed in eloquence, is reduced to the shouted single syllables of

> I say I love thee more than he can do.

The wrangle threatens a scrimmage, with Hermia in the middle of it. The equivoque and criss-cross of the writing here makes fine turmoil. They all fling at each other—as might four smart players at tennis keep the ball flying—till the lead of the scene next passes to Hermia—poor Hermia, brought up against the amazing fact that she and Helena have shifted places and that it is she who is now

> . . . miserable most, to love unlov'd.

Not that she sits down to mourn the matter.

> O me! you juggler! you canker-blossom!
> You thief of love! what, have you come by night,
> And stol'n my love's heart from him?

And—oh, what must Oberon be thinking as he watches!—instead of a gentlemanly fight, we are likely to have a most unladylike one. Another turn of the kaleidoscope. In place of Hermia making peace between the two young men we have Helena sconced between them for safety. And it must be owned that she takes advantage of it:

LYS. Be not afraid: she shall not harm thee, Helena.
DEM. No, sir; she shall not, though you take her part.
HEL. O, when she's angry, she is keen and shrewd:
  She was a vixen when she went to school;
  And, though she be but little, she is fierce.

But fortunately Demetrius and Lysander precipitate the one affair by marching off to fight in seemly solitude, and Helena, her protectors gone, as appropriately precipitates the other by running away.

Then Oberon can vent his anger upon Puck. But the passage that follows abounds in beauty besides. The tangles are unravelling, the fairy blessing impends. Puck, though, may have one more bout of fun.

> Up and down, up and down;
> I will lead them up and down:
> I am fear'd in field and town;
> Goblin, lead them up and down

From here to the scene's end note the variety of the metre, and how well it suits with the quick shifts and turns of the action. This rhythmic incantation, the broken couplets as Puck lures his two victims hither and

thither, the steadying or slowing of the verse as they
resign themselves to exhaustion and sleep (Lysander the
more mellifluously), the gentler beat in the more formal
stanzas for Helena and Hermia (sure signs, though, in
Hermia's of unabated temper), and, finally, Puck's pleasant little lullaby chant of appeasement.

> On the ground
> Sleep sound:
> I'll apply
> To your eye,
> Gentle lover, remedy.
> When thou wak'st,
> Thou tak'st
> True delight
> In the sight
> Of thy former lady's eye:
> And the country proverb known,
> That every man should take his own,
> In your waking shall be shown:
> Jack shall have Jill;
> Nought shall go ill;

The man shall have his mare again, and all shall be well.

No one, understanding the plain meaning of English
and having any ear at all, can possibly go wrong over
the speaking of that. It is as surely set to its own essential
music as if it were barred and scored.

Theseus and Hippolyta together form the play's centre
of gravity. The position in its very nature must forbid
overmuch activity, but of such as there is, he certainly
takes the hero's share.[21] He is not left quite a lay figure,
however. To the conventional furnishings of a romantic-
heroic part Shakespeare adds a kindly humour and some
mellowness of wisdom, the liker a true hero's as it is

carried lightly. His famous peroration upon the lunatic, the lover and the poet might merely serve to count him as one of them. But the less quoted snub to that snobbish Lord Chamberlain, Philostrate (and to Hippolyta also, one fears must be added; for with her wedding she seems to shed the last traces of Amazon and to turn Athenian—or Elizabethan—fine lady, top to toe) is more characteristic and, in its place, dramatically far more effective.

> Where I have come, great clerks have purposed
> To greet me with premeditated welcomes;
> Where I have seen them shiver and look pale,
> Make periods in the midst of sentences,
> Throttle their practis'd accent in their fears,
> And, in conclusion, dumbly have broke off,
> Not paying me a welcome. Trust me, sweet,
> Out of this silence yet I pick'd a welcome;
> And in the modesty of fearful duty
> I read as much as from the rattling tongue
> Of saucy and audacious eloquence.
> Love, therefore, and tongue-tied simplicity
> In least speak most, to my capacity.

This is kingly.

And if the play really was written for a wedding feast and was first played to brides, bridegrooms and guests, then the dovetailing of the interlude into the play and the making its audience a mirror and echo of the actual audience becomes a delightful dramatic device. Of this, we can, of course, recapture little or nothing of the effect; and the fairy benediction, once so charged with meaning, becomes, in the casual theatre, a matter of pleasant-sounding verse, hardly more.[22]

Shakespeare, it is to be feared, played somewhat false by the clowns. A clown is a rustic fellow, a townsman will call him a comic fellow. There is ample scope here for observant humour; so there is in the countryman's opinion of the townsman, could he make it articulate. Shakespeare knew enough of both town and country to play the honest broker between them. With Quince, Bottom and the rest he begins fairly enough. What could be more delightfully observant than their first assembly, than the rehearsal in the wood—or, indeed, than the mourning for Bottom's defection, or even than the beginning of the interlude itself? But in the theatre as he found it, there was the other sort of clown to be considered, the clown who played the clown; and, more often—as his antics have taught us now-a-days to express it—clowned the clown. And to the chief of these fell the character of Bottom. Therefore while it is partly the best thing in the play, it is, perhaps, partly the worst. Nor will it do to attribute its lapses (as we can, for instance, with the Fool in *King Lear*) to an actor speaking more than was set down for him—and having it set down. They are not, on the whole, of that robust and inconsiderate foolishness which marks the hail-fellow humour of the popular comedian. It is rather as if Shakespeare had felt upon this occasion that his actor would not be content without some dollops of the usual nonsense and had indifferently provided a few, leaving him to enrich them if he could—and doubtless he did! We have, in fact, now Bottom the Weaver and, again, Bottom the buffoon. We know, of course, that Shakespeare had fault to find with the comic actors of his day, though we may fairly weigh the kindlier reference to the clown in *Twelfth Night* against the more commonly quoted passage from *Hamlet*. But there is evidence from all sides that playwrights and judicious spectators both began to find the clowns a nuisance. There had begun, in fact, that never-ending battle of the drama against its actors—

though many an actor, no doubt, then as now, was valiantly on the drama's side. One difficulty was that the Clown, the 'all-licens'd Fool', had, so to speak, occupied the ground first, claiming a traditional right to his place there. His licence, expiring at Court, found yet fuller scope in the theatre. Not that Shakespeare had any fundamental grudge against him. In his legitimate motley, agile, a sweet singer, skilled on the pipe and tabor, he is given delightful employment in play after play. The difficulty would arise when comic *character* had to be interpreted. And this is a fundamental difficulty, and it remains to this day; it cannot perhaps ever be overcome. For your 'born comedian', your 'funny man' is only funny if he may be himself—exaggeratedly and ridiculously himself. If he lets that self be absorbed in an alien character, he is lost in every sense. He cannot, indeed, so yield himself, and a forced attempt to leaves him cramped and unhappy. It is unreasonable to complain. His art, of its sort, is a perfectly legitimate one. But if a dramatist wants to make full use of it, he must leave scope for the bubbling, irresponsible native humour and for the doing and even speaking of much more than it will be possible to set down. This art, though, for all the likeness, is not the art of the interpretative actor. And it is when Shakespeare provides a part such as Bottom the Weaver, which calls for interpretation, yet both leaves and does not leave scope for sheer funniment, yields it half-heartedly, yields it grudgingly, that trouble arises. Whether on this occasion Master Shakespeare lost his habitual good temper with Master William Kempe for playing the fool too outrageously, whether, as is more likely, Master Kempe was aggrieved to find his part (if he did play it) rather thin where there should have been most 'fat' in it, or whether this was not, as it happened, one of the provocations to the penning of that passage in *Hamlet*, it is useless to speculate. Our dilemma remains.[23]

We have the Bottom of the first two scenes, the rustic Roscius among his fellow rustics. He is not fooling; there is not a smile on his face, nor a twinkle in his eye. He faces his responsibilities—and everyone else's—with solid seriousness. Like a later amateur of legend, could he have been cast for Othello, he would have blacked himself all over. How did he scape—we fear the Duke was thrifty, and he did—that sixpence a day for life? This is, from the legitimate, the observantly humorous actor's point of view, the real thing, and he will know how to treat it. The passages with Titania are well enough; if neither Shakespeare nor any actor can make more of them it is mainly the fault of the ass-head with which both are burdened. But the waking from the dream is the thinnest and emptiest of stuff. Here, if the actor cannot somehow contrive to do more than the author has done, his audience must only wish that he could. And, as far as Bottom is concerned, the return to his sorrowing fellows is no better. Then, in the interlude itself, Shakespeare seems to say, after some hesitation, after extracting some genuine comedy from good Quince's tragedy, 'Oh, well, here you are'—

> Now am I dead,
> Now am I fled;
> My soul is in the sky.

This and more like it is not funny in the sense that the stuttering of the prologue, the innocence of Wall and Lion, Bottom's own aside to Theseus, are funny. It comes decidedly amiss. It is not the sort of thing that simpleness and duty tenders—and Shakespeare knew that well enough. Did he throw this bit of 'fat' to his comedian as a bone to a dog, that he, in turn, might throw it to the audience? He allots to his mock audience some specimens of the pretentious and even sillier jokes with which, presumably, such young sparks were wont to interrupt his own plays. Was that his sly revenge upon them for their greedy gobbling of the husks of his art as well as the good grain? Or—and it is likelier—did he do it all with a divine carelessness; as he would ever, it seems, make the most of a scene that came happily to life under his hand, let another hang limp if it wouldn't, and impenitently bolster up a third with mechanical foolery if the need were?

This, at least, is the case for the prosecution, Bottom in the dock. On all counts doubtless a defence can be set up. Bottom is ineffective when he awakes because he is still distraught with the enchantment. His jokes when he rejoins the despairing company are flavourless, because he is in haste and the interlude is impending. And some actual instance of such Arcadian artlessness as 'Now am I dead' can quite possibly be brought into evidence. This last, though, would be a poor aesthetic plea. And what cannot be argued away is the fact that the real fun of Bottom lies in the one set of scenes and not in the other.

To face our dilemma: when we stage the play, which sort of a clown is Bottom to be? Down to Charles Lamb and Hazlitt's day (and considerably later, though not with such credit) the tradition of the droll survived, and mummery and even gagging was allowable. But to-day we approach our Shakespeare hieratically, and the droll has been banished to the music-hall. It is in some ways a pity. Too solemn a reverence needs an antidote. But recall him and he would return an intimidated man, and nothing is duller than half-hearted foolery. Better then, at any rate where Bottom is concerned, give value to the part of him which Shakespeare, by every sign,

whole-heartedly liked writing—we shall get good value
from it—and let the rest go for what it may still prove
worth.

For the best of him, the simplest of him, is so irresis-
tibly good.

> An I may hide my face, let me play Thisby too.
> I'll speak in a monstrous little voice . . .

He is so earnest, so confident, so resolved on success,
so willing to bear the burden of it; and after all who
should, who can, but he? But Quince, the ever-tactful,
fends him off; then hurries—does he?—through his giving out the rest of the parts for fear lest yet another
should strike Bottom's fancy, till with relief he can turn
from Snug the joiner with

> I hope here is a play fitted.

If Snug could but have left well alone! Untimely dif-
fidence!

> Have you the lion's part written? pray you, if it be give it
> me, for I am slow of study.
> You may do it extempore, for it is nothing but roaring.

Quince has a pretty wit, a dry and academic wit. Surely
he is the author of the interlude. Is he not ready to turn
out a prologue in eight and six. But is this a time for
trifling? Bottom intervenes:

> Let me play the lion too: I will roar that I will do any
> man's heart good to hear me; I will roar that I will make
> the Duke say, 'Let him roar again, let him roar again.'

Quince returns to diplomacy, a twinkle in his eye.

> An you should do it too terribly you would fright the
> duchess and the ladies, that they would shriek; and that
> were enough to hang us all.

This tells—on the rest!

> That would hang us, every mother's son.

And who so conscious as Bottom of the risks they would run without him?

> I grant you, friends, if you should fright the ladies out of their wits, they would have no more discretion but to hang us: but I will aggravate my voice so, that I will roar you as gently as any sucking dove; I will roar you an 'twere any nightingale.

Whereat poor Quince loses his temper—and very nearly his leading actor too. Flattery may still save the situation; why ever be sparing of it?

> You can play no part but Pyramus: for Pyramus is a sweet faced man; a proper man, as one shall see in a summer's day; a most lovely, gentleman-like man; therefore you must needs play Pyramus.
> Well, I will undertake it.

After which turn of magnanimity they are all quite content to listen to a list of his fancies in that important matter of the beard he must wear.

This and the like of it is no foolery, but what better fun do we need? The kindly, crotchety, whimsical Quince, the modest Flute, the meek Snug, cautious Snout, amenable Starveling, with lordly Bottom to lead them! Sweet bully Bottom, the best wit of any handicraft man in Athens, with the best person, and a very paramour for a sweet voice! He can teach the Duke himself a thing or two about the theatre and how to behave there—and, being in his element, does!

If these are clowns, it is not in any motley sense. Rather they are the wholesomely humorously human foundation, without which the airy poetic structure of the play might well be too weak to stand.

Notes

1 Georg Brandes, *William Shakespeare: A Critical Study*, tr. William Archer, Mary Morison, and Diana White, London, 1914, p. 71 (orig. pub. 1898).

2 German dramatist (1761–1819) immensely popular throughout Europe. Benjamin Thompson translated and adapted several of his plays for Drury Lane around the turn of the 18th century. Sheridan adapted *Die Spanier in Peru* as *Pizarro* in 1799.

3 Popular English dramatist (1784–1862), a cousin of Sheridan and a friend of Hazlitt, Lamb, and Coleridge. He wrote many plays, including roles for Kean and Macready.

4 English dramatist (1796–1880), extremely prolific, remembered mainly for his work with the Vestris-Mathews management at the Lyceum.

5 From James Thompson's *Tragedy of Sophonisba* (1730), parodied by Fielding in *Tom Thumb*. The line was later changed to 'Oh, Sophonisba, I am wholly thine.' Johnson refers to the line in his life of Thompson in *Lives of the Poets*.

6 See the 1924 'Preface' to *A Midsummer Night's Dream*, pp. 50–51 and note 13.

7 There may even be a deep disharmony in an attempt to respond with sight and hearing simultaneously to any purely *emotional* appeal. In the theatre, of course, the two senses are under intellectual guidance—or should be. But this may be what is wrong—and there is something fundamentally wrong—with modern opera.

8 Not that conventions (in the theatre or elsewhere) are necessarily such rigid things as, untested, they may seem. Often we are unconsciously weary of them and ready enough to adopt a new one. By a little coaxing a lost one may be revived. By boldness the most formidable may sometimes be simply neglected. It is a producer's business to discern which—for his immediate purposes—have aesthetic validity and which have none.

9 Such an interval as the Folio directs between Acts III and IV of this play I call formal acceptance. By it the dramatist marks a certain rhythm in the play's action. An interval, in which an audience disperses or talks, has a further import-

ance. In a modern theatre this relaxing of attention, the breaking of the spell of emotion, an opportunity to make the passing of time seem more valid, are things to be seriously considered. How far these things affected Elizabethan audiences it is hard to say. But it is hard to believe that playwrights would remain insensible to the dramatic gain or loss that might be involved.

10 Some of these signs, being noted, have been interpreted as evidence of the play's original writing for a public theatre, the adaptation being for Court or wedding performance. But the Folio text is, hardly disputably, that of a prompt copy; and the stage-directions—for me the important evidence—are less likely to belong to a special performance than to the current practice of its acting. Though, again, this may, latterly, have been at a 'private' theatre—to which on all counts the play is better suited—rather than a public one.

11 This, of course, would be consistent with the play's original writing for the stage of a public theatre.

12 The stage arrangements at the 'private' theatres are still matters of discussion, and they may have approximated to this. But then the play's date comes into the question. If it was written for Shakespeare's company, where was it played if not either at their public theatre or in a private hall?

13 In his preface to *Music for A Midsummer Night's Dream*, Simpkin, Marshall, 1914.

14 And if there is such a thing as racial memory, music, one would say, could be counted on to call it to life.

15 Mr Richmond Noble, in his *Shakespeare's Use of Song*, holds that the song is not missing, and that 'Now until the break of day' and the twenty-two following lines *are* the song. I venture to disagree. The passage does not (but for the last three lines) differ in metre from much of the verse that is certainly meant to be spoken, as one would expect a lyric written for singing to do. Dramatically the context, Titania's

Will we sing and bless this place?

and Oberon's

Now, until the break of day

suggest a gap that some song has filled. Why 'Now', other-wise? And if Mr Noble's instinct, as he says—his musical instinct?—informs him that this passage is to be sung, my dramatic instinct suggests that its speaking by Oberon will give his part an ending commensurate with its importance. Singing alone might not detract from this, even though Oberon did little of the singing; but a ditty sung and danced certainly will. But then Mr Noble considers that

> Through the house give glimmering light

'must be either sung or intoned, otherwise the ascending value of the words cannot be adequately conveyed.' Could not as good reasons be found for treating half a dozen other passages in the same fashion? And are we not then on the road back to Mendelssohn's *recitative* for

> That very night I saw, but thou couldst not . . . ?

Incidentally Mr Noble condemns the use of

> *Roses, their sharp spines being gone,*

and denies it to Shakespeare. Upon the point of authorship I am no judge. But if its length is against it (one reason given), it is only one line longer than 'Now until the break of day' would be. And I should not have thought—speaking, again, under correction—that the opening phrases could be much more difficult to sing (another reason) than

> *You spotted snakes with double tongue,*
> *Thorny hedgehogs be not seen*, etc.,

must prove.

16 Not to mention that Bottom undertakes to roar us as gentle as any sucking dove!

17 It could be pedantically argued that neither Hermia's nor Helena's eyes were anointed with the love-juice; they, there-fore, might have behaved just a little more sensibly. This only shows the danger of ever starting to argue about *A Midsummer Night's Dream*.

18 By 'trick', needless to say, I, in no case, mean to imply anything 'tricky'.

19   The whole question of the employment of children on the stage is a difficult one. The social aspect of it cannot be touched on here. As to the artistic aspect: a self-conscious child is an abomination, and an unselfconscious child romping happily about is apt—even as a beautiful animal will—to make his elder companions look distressingly sophisticated and artificial. Age is a rough measurement in such matters, but one might say that from twelve to fifteen children are susceptible to training and can travel as far in the art as training can take them—which is not very far. Though again, base a complete performance upon training alone and it may be an excellent one, a far more enjoyable one than poor interpretation will produce. At fifteen, one may say, a child becomes capable of interpreting character, crudely or simply enough at first. Thereafter, artistically, he may grow up, or he may merely grow older.

20   And this applies, needless to say, with double force to the more important characters in the play; the actors of them must have mastered these things before the characters can come into question at all.

21   One of those dangerous moments, that are dear to the heart of the actor as providing (some recompense!) more amusement for him than the audience, is to be found—and circumvented—when in the first scene Theseus turns to the apparently long-forgotten Hippolyta with 'What cheer, my love'. It is open to the poor lady to revenge herself soundly upon Shakespeare by responding with a meaning smile. Thus does one enliven dull rehearsals.

22   Can we detect, too, Shakespeare's own mock apology for the imperfections of his work, put into the mouth of Theseus? Did Shakespeare, by any remote chance, play the part himself? It was in his line, according to tradition, and, if so, the joke would have been a good one indeed.

        Marry, if he that writ it, had play'd Pyramus, and hanged himself in Thisbe's garter, it would have been a fine tragedy.

23   Is no combination of the two sorts of comedy possible? This may well have been Shakespeare's own exasperated question.

Yes, every now and then, a peculiarly sympathetic and sensitive, a two-sided talent will be an exception to the rule. Did Shakespeare find, or think he had found, such a one to play the Fool in *King Lear*? 'Think' must be added; for whence came a few of those lines that smear the play?

The Winter's Tale

THESE FEW PREFACES make no pretence to Shakespearean scholarship, as that is usually understood. They are
only the elaborated notes of the producer, who must
view the play, first and last, as in action and on the
stage. But it is, after all, a normal way to view it.

The Winter's Tale belongs to the final period of Shakespeare's work; it is essentially a product of middle age; it
is a tragi-comedy. The technique of it is mature, that of
a man who knows he can do what he will, lets himself
in for difficulties with apparent carelessness, and over-
comes them at his ease. But if this is a masterpiece, one
questions several essentials of its making. One may
wonder first at the break in the interest made by the
passing of sixteen years. To a comedy this would be
deadening; for in comedy, no doubt, the closer the action
the better. To a tragedy it might be fatal; for, once well
started, a tragedy must not relax tension. But in a
tragi-comedy, as this is, is it not just some such jar that
is needed to break the play from the one mood to the
other? One may wonder at 'Time, as Chorus'. But it
must have pleased Shakespeare, I think, to use once
more, with mature skill, a device of his prentice days.
Masters of their art are apt to enjoy doing this. And it
is contrived that Time, in the middle of the play, shall
definitely strike that note of tolerant understanding, the
keynote of the whole play. A lesser artist, writing so,
might stray towards indifference or cynicism; Shakespeare can sustain the tone of it beautifully. The very
artifice of the device, moreover, attunes us to the artifice
of the story; saves us, at this dangerous juncture, when
Hermione is apparently dead, Antigonus quite certainly

eaten by the bear, from the true tragic mood. Moreover, 'Time, as Chorus', is the simple way to bridge dramatically the sixteen years, and therefore the right one.

There is more than one touch in the first half of the play, designed, I believe, to keep the tragedy a little less than tragic. Leontes' jealousy is never, as is Othello's, a strength, even a seeming strength (though of that comparison more in a minute); it is even less than a spiritual—it is a nervous weakness, a mere hysteria. He, poor wretch, moreover, even at his most positive, even while he sits in dignity and talks of justice, is conscious of this. After the one outbreak of rage with her, he never looks Hermione in the face, not through her trial, never until she has swooned. The man is a very drunkard of passion. Only in a passion of anger or cruelty, cold or hot, can he be sure of himself at all. Let him relax, and he is, as he says, a feather for each wind that blows. And the scene, coming nearest to true tragedy, where the babe is condemned to exposure, is yet heavily salted with the comedy of Paulina and Antigonus. At its height it becomes a slanging match. Was ever a character better contrived to keep the tragi-comic balance than Paulina? Little dignity is left to Leontes; and when any is restored to the scene, it is to Antigonus it falls as he takes the child in his arms to depart. Even in the scene of the trial when the tyrant breaks down under the sudden swift punishment of his folly, there is something a little ridiculous in his breathless confession to the surrounding courtiers, his frantic promises to undo what he has done. Paulina, too, relaxes from her high-toned scolding to an almost motherly fussiness, and the scene ends in pathos not in tragedy. But is it not this slight touch of the ridiculous which keeps it very human, and holds our sympathy; while the very suddenness of the catastrophe leaves us, paradoxically enough, expectant of some happier solution? Hardened into the finality of tragedy, the whole business would simply be too odious.

I believe there were three chief opportunities that Shakespeare saw in the old story of Dorastus and Fawnia. The first was this character of Leontes. Not so long before he had written *Othello*. *Othello* is popularly supposed now to be a study of jealousy, and probably was so thought and spoken of then. But as Dostoievsky points out (or rather points out that Pushkin points it out; but I have never read Pushkin) this is not so. It is the study of a primitive and noble nature, building its happiness upon a civilized ideal, and of the catastrophe that follows destruction of that ideal. Perhaps even Shakespeare himself had thought that jealousy was the centre-point of the *Othello* tragedy. It is a not uncommon thing for authors to set out with one scheme and complete another; he in particular was always building better than he knew when he began to build. Either way I imagine him seeing in Leontes a chance to retrieve that magnificent error, if error it was. If before he had set out to paint jealousy as a noble passion, and his own genius had defeated the false aim, now he would write a study of jealousy indeed, perverse, ignoble, pitiable.

Straightway he faced the first difficulty. Jealousy upon any foundation is less than jealousy, or more. Leontes has, as far as we can see, hardly the shadow of an excuse for his suspicion. Straightway he redeemed the blunder of Iago, that outrageous exhibition of theatrical virtuosity, redeemed it by writing this time no such character. That niche in the scheme is left vacant; and yet not vacant, but finely filled, for the wanton malice that is Iago the jealous man can only find, but finds surely, in his own heart.

The second opportunity in the play was, of course, the sheep-shearing scenes. Since the writing of *Henry IV*, Part

II, he had not been able to bring English country life into the theatre to any purpose; not since *A Midsummer Night's Dream* had his simple rustics had their full fling. To Leontes' Sicilian Court enough foreign colour is conscientiously given in descriptions of Delphi, mention of the warlike Smalus, and the like; but Bohemia is pure Warwickshire, and there are signs that Autolycus was something of a portrait. 'He married a widow not ten miles off, and compassed a motion of the Prodigal Son', looks very like it. Though it is the merest fancy, I like to think of Shakespeare happening on that puppet-play at Stratford Fair, and on his Autolycus behind it. And if only Autolycus had brought it with him to the Bohemian sheep-shearing! Punch and Judy is the only motion left to compass nowadays, and that is dying. Has anyone ever the heart to pass one by?

The third chance, I think, that Shakespeare saw and seized was the last scene of all, with Hermione as a statue. The crude stage effect is so good that hasty naked handling might have spoiled it. Raw material at its richest is also the hardest to work in. But Shakespeare goes about the business with great care. He prepares the audience, through Paulina's steward, almost to the pitch of revelation, saving just so much surprise, and leaving so little, that when they see the statue they may think themselves more in doubt than they really are whether it is Hermione herself or no. He prepares Leontes, who feels that his wife's spirit might walk again; who is startled by the strange air of Hermione that the yet unknown Perdita breathes out; who, his egotism killed, has become simple of speech, simple-minded, receptive. The scene is elaborately held back by the preceding one, which though but preparation, actually equals it in length, and its poetry is heightened by such contrast with fantastic prose and fun. While from the moment the statue is disclosed, every device of changing colour and time, every minor contrast of voice and mood that can give the scene modelling and beauty of form, is brought into easy use. Then the final effect of the music, of the brisk stirring trumpet sentences in Paulina's speech, of the simplicity of Leontes' 'let it be an act lawful as eating'. Then the swift contrast of the alarmed and sceptical Polixenes and Camillo, then Paulina's happiness breaking almost into chatter. And then the perfect sufficiency of Hermione's eight lines (oh, how a lesser dramatist might have overdone it with Noble Forgiveness and what not!)—it all really is a wonderful bit of work. And, as the play is ending, I know few things that move me more than—

> I, an old turtle,
> Will wing me to some wither'd bough and there
> My mate, that's never to be found again,
> Lament till I am lost.

Plucky Paulina; such a good fellow! Her sudden betrothal to precise old Camillo may seem queer to us dramatic realists, but such symmetry was as natural to an Elizabethan dramatist as was the rhetorical final speech without which he would no more have ended his play than would a classical musician now finish a symphony without a full close.

One could draw out the parallel between *The Winter's Tale* and *Othello* by the very close comparison to be made between Hermione and Paulina, and Desdemona and Emilia. Paulina is certainly a better done figure than Emilia, and though interest is not centred throughout on Hermione (nor is it on Leontes, and for this reason only I think has the play been less popular with our leading actors), she is to me a most attractive and, for a 'good' woman, a remarkably interesting figure. 'Goodness' in drama is too apt to become a merely negative quality. But the poet-dramatist has the advantage of being able to clothe such characters in great verbal beauty. And beyond that in Hermione (and that is much) I seem to see an exquisitely sensitive woman, high-minded, witty too, and tactful. She had been under no illusions about Leontes, had questioned herself carefully before marrying him; since then had made his court a gracious, happy place, and to do that could have been no easy matter. One can tell that she knows the danger of the man, but when the outrageous blow has fallen, even in her utter helplessness, she has perfect courage. Against all the trouble facing her she stands serene; only the cruel side-blow of her son's death fells her. Even then she falls silently, proudly still. And Perdita! Though it may be only delightful girlishness as seen from middle-aged manhood, it is none the less delightful. No play of Shakespeare's boasts three such women as Hermione, Perdita, Paulina.

One notes the touched-in resemblances between mother and daughter, father and son. Polixenes and Florizel, light-hearted, impetuous, inconsiderate both. Perdita, with all her mother's courage and self-possession, which, at sixteen, is obstinacy too. And there are many other fascinatingly clever touches that go to make up the complexity of Leontes. There is a most daring piece of technique by which twice or three times an actual obscurity of words (their meaning could never have been plain to any immediate listener) is used to express the turmoil of his mind. Even the little scene of Cleomenes and Dion returning with the oracle is a model 'bridge' from the raucous revilings of Leontes over the helpless child to the dignity of the scene of the trial.

I make no contribution to the controversy over the division of the plays into acts and scenes. Whether they were first divided by Shakespeare himself or by a later hand I have no idea, though in some cases (not that of *The Winter's Tale*) the division is quite badly done. It is possible that the developing structure of the theatre and the stage gradually made the scene-division both an easier and a more important matter; and possibly in Shakespeare's own case, at least, the increasing length of the later plays necessitated pauses. But that any and every Elizabethan play, and drama of rhetoric and the platform stage, should be played as swiftly and uninterruptedly as possible—of that I have not the shadow of doubt. Therefore for *The Winter's Tale* I make the obvious and natural division into two parts, and allow for the one pause only.

How should the play be costumed? I was happy to find myself at one with Albert Rothenstein about this. Not in classic dress certainly. No matter for Apollo's oracle and Leontes, Tyrant of Sicily; it would offend against the very spirit of the play. But—just to give one's imagination the key—Renaissance-classic, that is, classic dress as Shakespeare saw it, would be the thing. And when we had quite made up our minds to this I suddenly thought and said to Rothenstein, 'Giulio Romano! There's our pattern designer recommended in the play itself.' It's little I know of Giulio Romano. Ought I to confess that Rothenstein could remember little more? But Giulio Romano was looked up, and there the costumes were much as we had forethought them. For the Bohemian countryside let us fetter ourselves as little as Shakespeare did.

As to scenery, as scenery is mostly understood—canvas, realistically painted—I would have none of it. Decoration?—Yes. The difference is better seen than talked of, so I leave Norman Wilkinson's to be seen.

1912

Twelfth Night

THIS PLAY is classed, as to the period of its writing, with *Much Ado About Nothing*, *As You Like It*, and *Henry V*. But however close in date, in spirit I am very sure it is far from them. I confess to liking those other three as little as any plays he ever wrote. I find them so stodgily good, even a little (dare one say it?) vulgar, the work of a successful man who is caring most for success. I can imagine the lovers of his work losing hope in the Shakespeare of that year or two. He was thirty-five and the first impulse of his art had spent itself. He was popular. There was welcome enough, we may be sure, for as many *Much Ado's* and *As You Like It's* and jingo history pageants as he'd choose to manufacture. It was a turning point and he might have remained a popular dramatist. But from some rebirth in him that mediocre satisfaction was foregone, and, to our profit at least, came *Hamlet*, *Macbeth*, *Lear*, and the rest. *Hamlet*, perhaps, was popular, though Burbage may have claimed a just share in making it so. But I doubt if the great heart of the public would beat any more constantly towards the rarer tragedies in that century and society than it will in this. To the average man or playgoer three hundred or indeed three thousand years are as a day. While we have Shakespeare's own comment even on that 'supporter to a state', Polonius (true type of the official mind. And was he not indeed Lord Chamberlain?), that where art is concerned 'He's for a jig, or a tale of bawdry, or he sleeps.'

Twelfth Night is, to me, the last play of Shakespeare's golden age. I feel happy ease in the writing, and find much happy carelessness in the putting together. It is akin to the *Two Gentlemen of Verona* (compare Viola and

Julia), it echoes a little to the same tune as the sweeter parts of the *Merchant of Venice*, and its comic spirit is the spirit of the Falstaff scenes of *Henry IV*, that are to my taste the truest comedy he wrote.

There is much to show that the play was designed for performance upon a bare platform stage without traverses or inner rooms or the like. It has the virtues of this method, swiftness and cleanness of writing and simple directness of arrangement even where the plot is least simple. It takes full advantage of the method's convenience. The scene changes constantly from anywhere suitable to anywhere else that is equally so. The time of the play's action is any time that suits the author as he goes along. Scenery is an inconvenience. I am pretty sure that Shakespeare's performance went through without a break. Certainly its conventional arrangement into five acts for the printing of the Folio is neither by Shakespeare's nor any other sensitive hand; it is shockingly bad. If one must have intervals (as the discomforts of most theatres demand), I think the play falls as easily into the three divisions I have marked as any. [Intervals after II, iii and IV, i.]

I believe the play was written with a special cast in mind. Who was Shakespeare's clown, a sweet-voiced singer and something much more than a comic actor? He wrote Feste for him, and later the Fool in *Lear*. At least, I can conceive no dramatist risking the writing of such parts unless he knew he had a man to play them. And why a diminutive Maria—Penthesilea, the youngest wren of nine—unless it was only that the actor of the part was to be such a very small boy? I have cudgelled my brains to discover why Maria, as Maria, should be tiny, and finding no reason have ignored the point.

I believe too (this is a commonplace of criticism) that the plan of the play was altered in the writing of it.

Shakespeare sets out upon a passionate love romance, perseveres in this until (one detects the moment, it is that jolly midnight revel) Malvolio, Sir Toby and Sir Andrew completely capture him. Even then, perhaps, Maria's notable revenge on the affectioned ass is still to be kept within bounds. But two scenes later he begins to elaborate the new idea. The character of Fabian is added to take Feste's share of the rough practical joke and set him free for subtler wit. Then Shakespeare lets fling and works out the humorous business to his heart's content. That done, little enough space is left him if the play is to be over at the proper hour, and, it may be (if the play was being prepared for an occasion, the famous festivity in the Middle Temple Hall or another), there was little enough time to finish writing it in either. From any cause, we certainly have a scandalously ill-arranged and ill-written last scene, the despair of any stage manager. But one can discover, I believe, amid the chaos scraps of the play he first meant to write. Olivia suffers not so much by the midway change of plan, for it is about her house that the later action of the play proceeds, and she is on her author's hands. It is on Orsino, that interesting romantic, that the blow falls.

> Why should I not, had I the heart to do it,
> Like to the Egyptian thief at point of death,
> Kill what I love?—a savage jealousy
> That sometime savours nobly.

On that fine fury of his—shamefully reduced to those few lines—I believe the last part of the play was to have hung. It is too good a theme to have been meant to be so wasted. And the revelation of Olivia's marriage to his page (as he supposes), his reconciliation with her, and the more vital discovery that his comradely love for Viola is worth more to him after all than any high-sounding passion, is now all muddled up with the final rounding off of the comic relief. The character suffers severely. Orsino remains a finely interesting figure; he might have been a magnificent one. But there, it was Shakespeare's way to come out on the other side of his romance.

The most important aspect of the play must be viewed, to view it rightly, with Elizabethan eyes. Viola was played, and was meant to be played, by a boy. See what this involves. To that original audience the strain of make-believe in the matter ended just where for us it most begins, at Viola's entrance as a page. Shakespeare's audience saw Cesario without effort as Orsino sees him; more importantly they saw him as Olivia sees him; indeed it was over Olivia they had most to make believe. One feels at once how this affects the sympathy and balance of the love scenes of the play. One sees how dramatically right is the delicate still grace of the dialogue between Orsino and Cesario, and how possible it makes the more outspoken passion of the scenes with Olivia. Give to Olivia, as we must do now, all the value of her sex, and to the supposed Cesario none of the value of his, we are naturally quite unmoved by the business. Olivia looks a fool. And it is the common practice for actresses of Viola to seize every chance of reminding the audience that they are girls dressed up, to impress on one moreover, by childish by-play as to legs and petticoats or the absence of them, that this is the play's supreme joke. Now Shakespeare has devised one most carefully placed soliloquy where we are to be forcibly reminded that Cesario is Viola; in it he has as carefully divided the comic from the serious side of the matter. That scene played, the Viola, who does not do her best, as far as the passages with Olivia are concerned, to make us believe, as Olivia believes, that she is a man, shows, to my mind, a lack of imagination and is guilty of dramatic bad manners, knocking, for the sake of a little laughter, the whole of the play's romantic plot on the head.

Let me explain briefly the interpretation I favour of four or five other points.

I do not think that Sir Toby is meant for nothing but a bestial sot. He is a gentleman by birth, or he would not be Olivia's uncle (or cousin, if that is the relationship). He has been, it would seem, a soldier. He is a drinker, and while idleness leads him to excess, the boredom of Olivia's drawing-room, where she sits solitary in her mourning, drives him to such jolly companions as he can find: Maria and Fabian and the Fool. He is a poor relation, and has been dear to Sir Andrew some two thousand strong or so (poor Sir Andrew), but as to that he might say he was but anticipating his commission as matrimonial agent. Now, dull though Olivia's house may be, it is free quarters. He is, it seems, in some danger of losing them, but if only by good luck he could see Sir Andrew installed there as master! Not perhaps all one could wish for in an uncle; but to found an interpretation of Sir Toby only upon a study of his unfortunate surname is, I think, for the actor to give us both less and more than Shakespeare meant.

I do not believe that Sir Andrew is meant for a cretinous idiot. His accomplishments may not quite stand to Sir Toby's boast of them; alas! the three or four languages, word for word without book, seem to end at 'Dieu vous garde, Monsieur'. But Sir Andrew, as he would be if he could—the scholar to no purpose, the fine fellow to no end, in short the perfect gentleman—is still the ideal of better men than he who yet can find nothing better to do. One can meet a score of Sir Andrews, in greater or less perfection, any day after a

96

West End London lunch, doing, what I believe is called, a slope down Bond.

Fabian, I think, is not a young man, for he hardly treats Sir Toby as his senior, he is the cautious one of the practical jokers, and he has the courage to speak out to Olivia at the end. He treats Sir Andrew with a certain respect. He is a family retainer of some sort; from his talk he has to do with horses and dogs.

Feste, I feel, is not a young man either. There runs through all he says and does that vein of irony by which we may so often mark one of life's self-acknowledged failures. We gather that in those days, for a man of parts without character and with more wit than sense, there was a kindly refuge from the world's struggle as an allowed fool. Nowadays we no longer put them in livery.

I believe Antonio to be an exact picture of an Elizabethan seaman-adventurer, and Orsino's view of him to be just such as a Spanish grandee would have taken of Drake. 'Notable pirate' and 'salt-water thief', he calls him.

> A bawbling vessel was he captain of,
> For shallow draught and bulk unprizable;
> With which such scathful grapple did he make
> With the most noble bottom of our fleet,
> That very envy and the tongue of loss
> Cried fame and honour on him.

And Antonio is a passionate fellow as those west countrymen were. I am always reminded of him by the story of Richard Grenville chewing a wineglass in his rage.

The keynotes of the poetry of the play are that it is passionate and it is exquisite. It is life, I believe, as Shakespeare glimpsed it with the eye of his genius in that half-Italianized court of Elizabeth. Orsino, Olivia,

Antonio, Sebastian, Viola are passionate all, and conscious of the worth of their passion in terms of beauty. To have one's full laugh at the play's comedy is no longer possible, even for an audience of Elizabethan experts. Though the humour that is set in character is humour still, so much of the salt of it, its play upon the time and place, can have no savour for us. Instead we have learned editors disputing over the existence and meaning of jokes at which the simplest soul was meant to laugh unthinkingly. I would cut out nothing else, but I think I am justified in cutting those pathetic survivals.

Finally, as to the speaking of the verse and prose. The prose is mostly simple and straightforward. True, he could no more resist a fine-sounding word than, as has been said, he could resist a pun. They abound, but if we have any taste for the flavour of a language he makes us delight in them equally. There is none of that difficult involuted decoration for its own sake in which he revelled in the later plays. The verse is still regular, still lyrical in its inspiration, and it should I think be spoken swiftly . . .

I think that all Elizabethan dramatic verse must be spoken swiftly, and nothing can make me think otherwise. My fellow workers acting in *The Winter's Tale* were accused by some people (only by some) of gabbling. I readily take that accusation on myself, and I deny it. Gabbling implies hasty speech, but our ideal was speed, nor was the speed universal, nor, but in a dozen well-defined passages, really so great. Unexpected it was, I don't doubt; and once exceed the legal limit, as well accuse you of seventy miles an hour as twenty-one. But I call in question the evidence of mere policemen-critics. I question a little their expertness of hearing, a little too their quickness of understanding Elizabethan English not at its easiest, just a little their lack of delight in anything that is not as they thought it always would be, and I suggest that it is more difficult than they think to look and listen and remember and appraise all in the same flash of time. But be all the shortcomings on one side and that side ours, it is still no proof that the thing come short of is not the right thing. That is the important point to determine, and for much criticism that has been helpful in amending what we did and making clearer what we should strive towards—I tender thanks.

The Winter's Tale, as I see its writing, is complex, vivid, abundant in the variety of its mood and pace and colour, now disordered, now at rest, the product of a mind rapid, changing, and over-full. I believe its interpretation should express all that. *Twelfth Night* is quite other. Daily, as we rehearse together, I learn more what it is and should be; the working together of the theatre is a fine thing. But, as a man is asked to name his stroke at billiards, I will even now commit myself to this: its serious mood is passionate, its verse is lyrical, the speaking of it needs swiftness and fine tone; not rush, but rhythm, constant and compelling. And now I wait contentedly to be told that less rhythmic speaking of Shakespeare has never been heard.

1912

Notes

Notes

Notes

Notes